TWELVE MONTHS OF KNITTING

TWELVE MONTHS
OF KNITTING

36 PROJECTS TO KNIT YOUR WAY THROUGH THE YEAR

By Joanne Yordanou

PHOTOGRAPHY BY JENNIFER BURRELL

POTTER
CRAFT

NEW YORK

To Mom and Dad, who lovingly raised me to believe I can do anything I set my mind to. And to my husband, Lou, and our children, Lucy and Elizabeth, for your support and love.

Copyright © 2008 by Joanne Yordanou

Published in the United States by Potter Craft, an imprint of the
Crown Publishing Group, a division of Random House, Inc., New York.
www.crownpublishing.com
www.pottercraft.com

POTTER CRAFT and CLARKSON N. POTTER are trademarks, and POTTER
and colophon are registered trademarks of Random House, Inc.

Library of Congress Cataloging-in-Publication Data
Yordanou, Joanne, 1964-
Twelve months of knitting: 36 projects to knit your way through the year /
by Joanne Yordanou.—1st ed.   p. cm.

Includes index.
ISBN 978-0-307-35163-0
1. Knitting—Patterns. I. Title.
TT820.Y67 2008
746.43'2041--dc22
2007023310

Printed in China

Design by Chalkley Calderwood Pratt

Thanks to the Craft Yarn Council of America (www.yarnstandards.com)
for their Standard Yarn Weight System Chart, which appears on page 158.

10 9 8 7 6 5 4 3 2 1

First Edition

ACKNOWLEDGMENTS

THE THING ABOUT NEW EXPERIENCES is that they are ever-changing and evolving, and, like aging (or growing, depending on how you look at it), you are learning at the same time. With each experience, you are forced to learn the nuances of the business, sport, or genre. In writing a book, I have met many new people and developed new skills. These new acquaintances have taken me into their world. They gave me tips and comments without forcing their will, but gently helping me make this book the best I could—it is as much their book as it is mine. These people have become friends, which has made the writing of this book a richer experience than I could have wished for.

Marlene, you were the one so excited you picked up the phone, and we had that great conversation that began this

dream. You guided me to ensure I was ready to find a publisher. Thank you Marlene Connor! Who brought me to Rosy Ngo, whom I thank for believing in this idea of a book and taking it on. My search for a photographer brought me to Jen, who immediately saw what I saw and translated it into her photographs. I am grateful to know you as a colleague, but more importantly as a friend. You had plenty to deal with and remained always the professional. Doug, I don't know whether to thank you more for helping Lou build the deck or helping Jen, so I thank you for both!

I worked with Svetlana Avrakh at the Patons design studio and knew her to be an eagle-eyed technical editor and wonderful designer. Thank you for your dedication. Thanks to Gayle Ford, whose work I have admired in *Interweave Knits*, for her wonderful drawings. Each test knitter patiently knitted each design, some patterns easy and some gnarly, ironing out snags or helping me make it a better pattern. I am grateful and am always in awe of the brilliant women who knit for me. I give thanks to Joyce Murray, Dolly D'Costa, Francesca Gourgoin, Alina McQuarrie, Joan Kass, Pat McClymont, Olga Dohlan, Wannietta Prescod, Susannah MacRae, Kamla Sharma, Jessie McGregor, Isobel Watkinson, and April Cornell for their superb knitting. I am extremely thankful to have such a wonderful family and friends and am doubly fortunate to have some as models for this book. Chelsea, Sarah, Scott, Angela, Deb, Lucy, Elizabeth, Khoan, Margaret, Krystyn, Doug, Jules, Emma, and Liam—you all look super-fab and did a fantastic job! My thanks to the yarn companies who have generously contributed yarn to this book: Classic Elite Yarns, Needful Yarns, Spinrite (Patons & Lily), Crystal Palace, Westminster Fibres for Rowan, CNS Yarns for Mission Falls, Blue Sky Alpacas, Fleece Artist, SR Kertzer, Tahki/Stacy Charles, and Yarnopolis for Manos Del Uruguay—loved it all!

INTRODUCTION

I wouldn't call myself a crazy knitter or a knit-a-holic, unless you consider knitting hundreds and hundreds of 4" x 4" (10cm x 10cm) swatches crazy (maybe you would). But it's true—I love to knit swatches, trying many ideas and stitches out in small, or sometimes large, squares.

My passion is in the designing, and my excitement is with the color. My creative urge is satisfied when I design. I awaken at night with my best ideas, and until I get them on paper, I cannot go back to sleep. As it happens, I love to knit, so there my passion finds its outlet.

When I created Baa Baa Knits and Needleworks for selling online and at craft shows, it allowed me to design and publish my favorites. After five years of selling knitting and needlepoint kits, I decided to downscale the retail side of the business and concentrate on just designing. I am also a bit of a written word junkie, whether books or magazines. I also adore calendars and blank journals, which encourage me to write. So it has always been a dream of mine to write my own book. This book, *Twelve Months of Knitting*, is the realization of my desire to create beautiful sweaters and other knitted items with sumptuous yarn in a beautiful book.

One of the first questions from beginning knitters is "What do I knit?" This book offers patterns for all levels of knitters and will help develop the skills needed to advance to the next level. For example, you may come to this book with a basic knowledge of how to knit and purl. As you move through these projects, you will learn how to master cables or Fair Isle patterns. If you are an experienced knitter, perhaps you never grasped intarsia—you'll learn that here. Whatever your skill level, you will find tips throughout, which will guide you through new techniques and provide clear illustrations.

Knitting is not just a winter pastime. With the variety and choice we have in yarn today, knitting can be enjoyed year-round. How you use this book is up to you. You may want to do a project per month and work toward the end of the year. Or you may wish to jump around trying different designs in different months. You can plan your knitting using the planner (pages 10–11), which tells you when to begin the project for the month it represents. The calendar is only a guide, based on average knitting speed. Depending on how slowly or quickly you knit, you may decide to change the timing. As you work through these projects, I urge you to become a crazy swatcher, too. Taking the time to check your gauge for each project will ultimately save you time. And keep those swatches! When I retire, I plan to sew all my favorites into a blanket.

I hope you enjoy the designs and love knitting them!

Happy Knitting,
Joanne

Knitting is not just a winter pastime. With the variety we have in yarn today, knitting can be enjoyed year-round.

THE KNITTER'S WEEKLY PLANNER

This table will help you plan the knitting projects in this book. Given these general timelines for completion, you'll know when to start so your finished project can be worn at the right time of year.

	JAN	FEB	MARCH	APRIL	MAY	JUNE
WEEK 1	Boyfriend Sweater 3–4 wks PAGE 34		BVI Bikini 1 wk PAGE 43	Little Boy Blue 2 wks PAGE 62	Boat Launch Cables 3–4 wks PAGE 94	Rosseau Bandeau 1 wk PAGE 91
WEEK 2	Kiss Curls Snuggle Wrap 2–3 wks PAGE 30		Auction Cardie 2–4 wks PAGE 67	Bookworm Bookmark 1 wk PAGE 55	Dad's Neighborhood Cardigan 3-4 wks PAGE 83	Cottage Table Settings 2–3 wks PAGE 89
WEEK 3	Girl's Valentine Cardigan 2 wks PAGE 27	Holiday Beach Cover-Up 3–4 wks PAGE 46	Stitch Therapy Turtleneck 3–4 wks PAGE 57		Adirondack Lap Blanket 1–2 wks PAGE 78	
WEEK 4		Key West Cropped Top 1–2 wks PAGE 41	Flower Power Felted Bag 1–2 wks PAGE 52	Extraordinary Orchids Cardigan 4–5 wks PAGE 71		
WEEK 5				Cottage Socks 1 wk PAGE 80		

JULY	AUG	SEPT	OCT	NOV	DEC
College Daze 2–3 wks PAGE 115	Lace Pillows 1 wk each PAGE 102		Out in the Woods Sweater 4–5 wks PAGE 131	Evening Festivities Cardigan 3–4 wks PAGE 146	Ski Lodge Scoop 1–2 wks PAGE 14
Ode to Jackie O 3–4 wks PAGE 105	Fair Isle Vest 3–4 wks PAGE 118	Doggy Doodle 2 wks PAGE 128	49th Parallel Hats & Mitts 1–2 wks PAGE 137	Turtle Doves 1–2 wks PAGE 139	Ski Lodge Bag 1–2 wks PAGE 17
Summer Chill Shawl 3 wks PAGE 107		Wrist Warmers 1–3 days PAGE 112	Scarves to Impress 1–2 wks each PAGE 140	Red Cable Cardigan 3–4 wks PAGE 151	
	Kimono Wrap 1–2 wks PAGE 125			Cross-Country Ski Sweater and Hat 3–4 wks PAGE 18	

JANUARY

JANUARY IS THE QUIET MONTH. The festive season is over. Children are back in school. We are back to work, and the cocooning has begun. There is satisfaction in packing away decorations and getting back to routine. This is the month we steal time away for ourselves, after two or three months of shopping, decorating, cooking, and socializing. We need snippets of quietude in corners, to cast on a few stitches.

The hurly burly month of December has ended and we have grabbed the luxury of time back for ourselves. We pick just the right day-timer, calendar, or journal from a choice of many. This could take hours and then, in it, we make our new year's resolutions to manage our time better. Or you might plan out your year of knitting: gifts to knit for next Christmas, summer or travel projects, and all of those things to get done before next year. You might begin an exercise program or reclaim your favorite chair by the window for your "knitting by a snowy window" evening.

January is the month for new beginnings, reflections and goals. Is it your goal to do one project a month from this book? Or to hone your knitting skills by working at the projects that target your limitations. Have you always wanted to make socks? Or tackled an all-over cabled sweater? Set goals that are attainable, but stretch your skills slightly. You will be rewarded.

14

17

18

Opportunity is missed by most people because it is dressed in overalls and looks like work.
—THOMAS EDISON
(1847–1931)

Ski Lodge Scoop

The tall ribbing brings a sense of modernity to this simple knit. I could easily knit three scoops for my wardrobe in different colors—and three matching bags!

Beginner

SIZE
Small (Medium, Large)

Bust and finished size: 30 (34, 36)" (76 [86.5, 91.5]cm)

MATERIALS
3 (4, 4) hanks Manos del Uruguay wool (3½ oz [100g]/ 138 yds [126m]; 100% wool), #106 Red, 🌀 medium

NOTE Because of the distinctive tones of each skein, it is recommended that you work 2 rows from one skein and then 2 rows from another skein to even out the dyes.

1 pair US sizes 8 (5mm) needles

1 pair US size 9 (5.5mm) needles or size required to achieve gauge

2 stitch holders

GAUGE
16 stitches and 24 rows = 4" (10cm) in stockinette stitch with US 9 (5.5mm) needles

Note The instructions are written for the smallest size. When changes are necessary for larger sizes, those instructions are enclosed in parentheses.

Back

**With larger needles, cast on 70 (86, 90) stitches.

Row 1 (RS) K2, *p2, k2; repeat from * to end of row.

Row 2 P2, *k2, p2; repeat from * to end of row.

Repeat rows 1–2 until the Back measures 10" (25.5cm) from the cast-on edge, ending with RS facing for next row and decreasing 10 (18, 18) stitches evenly across last row—60 (68, 72) stitches.

Work 3" (7.5cm) in stockinette stitch, ending with RS facing for next row.

ARMHOLE SHAPING

Bind off 3 stitches at the beginning of the next 2 rows— 54 (62, 66) stitches.

Decrease 1 stitch at each end of the needle on every RS row 2 (2, 3) times. 50 (58, 60) stitches.**

Continue even until the Back measures 21½" (54.5cm) from the cast-on edge, ending with RS facing for next row.

SHOULDER SHAPING

Bind off 6 (7, 7) stitches at the beginning of the next 2 rows, then bind off 7 (7, 8) stitches at the beginning of the following 2 rows. Leave the remaining 24 (30, 30) stitches on a stitch holder for the Back neck.

Front

Work from ** to ** as for the Back.

Continue in stockinette stitch until the armhole measures 2" (5cm), ending with RS facing for next row.

NECK SHAPING (LEFT SIDE)

K21 (25, 26), turn. Leave remaining stitches on a spare needle.

Decrease 1 stitch at the neck edge on the next 3 (5, 5) rows, then every 2nd row 5 (6, 6) times—13 (14, 15) stitches.

Continue even until the Front measures 21½" (54.5cm) from the cast-on edge, ending with RS facing for next row.

SHOULDER SHAPING (LEFT SIDE)

Bind off 6 (7, 7) stitches at the beginning of the next row. Work 1 row even. Bind off the remaining 7 (7, 8) stitches.

NECK SHAPING (RIGHT SIDE)

With RS facing, slip 8 stitches off the spare needle onto a stitch holder. Join yarn to the remaining stitches, and decrease 1 stitch at the neck edge on the next 3 (5, 5) rows, then every 2nd row 5 (6, 6) times—13 (14, 15) stitches.

Continue even until the Front measures 21½" (54.5cm) from the cast-on edge, ending with WS facing for next row.

SHOULDER SHAPING (RIGHT SIDE)

Bind off 6 (7, 7) stitches at the beginning of the next row. Work 1 row even. Bind off the remaining 7 (7, 8) stitches.

Finishing

Block the pieces to the measurements. Sew the left shoulder seam.

NECK BAND

With RS facing and smaller needles, pick up and knit 31 stitches down the left Front neck edge. Knit 8 stitches from the stitch holder. Pick up and knit 31 stitches up the right Front neck edge. Knit 24 (30, 30) stitches from the Back neck stitch holder. 96 (102, 102) stitches. Work 6 rows in k2, p2 ribbing as given for the Back. Bind off in ribbing (RS).

ARMBANDS

Sew the right shoulder seam. With RS facing and smaller needles, pick up and knit 82 stitches around the armhole. Work 6 rows in k2, p2 ribbing as given for the Back. Bind off in ribbing (RS).

Sew the side seams.

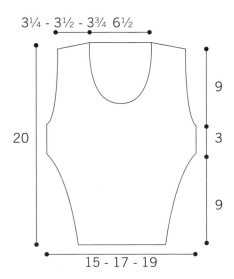

3¼ - 3½ - 3¾ 6½

9

3

9

20

15 - 17 - 19

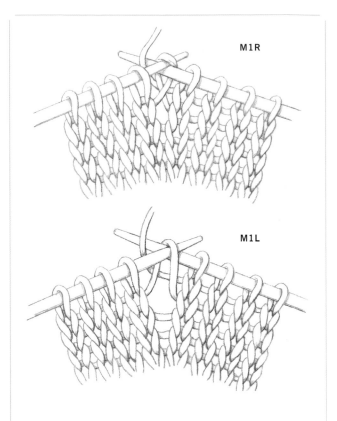

M1R

M1L

Increasing Stitches

The first increase we usually learn is the bar increase, in which you knit into the front and back of the stitch. It's named for the horizontal bar it creates that visibly underlines the new stitch. This is great to use at seams, but to have a less obvious increase, use the "make one" increase instead:

M1R (MAKE ONE RIGHT)

With the left-hand needle, pick up the strand that lies between the stitches *from back to front*. With right-hand needle, knit this stitch.

M1L (MAKE ONE LEFT)

With left-hand needle, pick up the strand that lies between the stitches *from front to back*. With right-hand needle, knit into *back* of this stitch.

Ski Lodge Bag

The Ski Lodge Bag can go solo as a funky bag to take anywhere.

Intermediate

MATERIALS

2 hanks Manos del Uruguay wool (3½ oz [100g]/138 yds [126m]; 100% wool), #106 Red, (4) medium

<u>NOTE</u> Because of the distinctive tones of each skein, work 2 rows from one skein and then 2 rows from another skein to even out the dyes on the work.

1 pair US 9 (5.5mm) needles or size required to achieve gauge

1 set US 9 (5.5mm) double-pointed needles

2 stitch holders

GAUGE

16 stitches and 24 rows = 4" (10cm) in stockinette stitch

Bag

Cast on 88 stitches.

Work 4 rows in stockinette stitch, increasing 14 stitches evenly across the last row—102 stitches.

Rows 5–7 *K2, p2; repeat from * to end of row.

Row 8 (WS) Knit.

Row 9 (Eyelet Row) K2, *k2tog, yfwd, k2; repeat from * to end of row.

Row 10 Knit.

Continue in ribbing for 8" (20.5cm) more, ending with WS facing for next row.

Next row (WS) Purl, decreasing 12 stitches evenly across the row—90 stitches. PM (place marker).

Work 4 rows in stockinette stitch. PM.

BOTTOM SHAPING

Row 1 (RS) K2, *k2tog, k9; repeat from * to end of row—82 stitches.

Row 2 and all other WS rows Purl.

Row 3 K2, *k2tog, k8; repeat from * to end of row—74 stitches.

Row 5 K2, *k2tog, k7; repeat from * to end of row—66 stitches.

Continue in this manner, decreasing 8 stitches every alternate row until there are 10 stitches remaining. Break yarn, leaving a long end. Thread the yarn through the remaining stitches and pull to secure. Weave in the end.

With WS facing, sew the rows together between the markers to form a rolled edge. Sew the side seam.

I-CORD STRAP

With double-pointed needles, cast on 4 stitches. *Do not turn. With RS facing, slide these 4 stitches to the other end of the needle. Pull tight and knit these 4 stitches.

Repeat from * until the cord measures 58" (147.5cm) or desired length. Bind off on RS. Thread the strap through the eyelet row and tie in a knot.

I-Cord

I-cord is easy to make. It makes great hooks and handles for anything.

Cross-Country Ski Sweater and Hat

This yarn is so soft and warm, you can't help touching it. The sweater was inspired by the Norwegian après-ski look. Whether cross-country or alpine skiing—or just looking good in the chalet—prepare to have people touching you while you're wearing it.

Experienced

SIZE

SWEATER

Bust: 30–32 (34–36, 38–40, 42–44)" (76–81.5 [86.5–91.5, 96.5–101.5, 106.5–112]cm)

Finished size: 36½ (40, 45, 47)" (92.5 [101.5, 114.5, 119.5]cm)

HAT

To fit a 21" (53.5cm) head

MATERIALS

Classic Elite Yarns Lush (1¾ oz [50g]/104 yds [95m]; 50% Angora/50% Wool), (3) light

   12 hanks #4407 Thistle (MC)

   1 hank #4474 Keys Green (A)

   1 hank #4416 Natural (B)

1 pair US 6 (4mm) needles

1 set US 6 (4mm) double-pointed needles

1 pair US 7 (4.5mm) needles or size required to achieve gauge

1 set US 7 (4.5mm) double-pointed needles

1 cable needle

3 stitch holders

GAUGE

16 stitches and 24 rows = 4" (10cm) in stockinette stitch with larger needles

22 stitches and 22 rows = 4" (10cm) in cable pattern with larger needles

STITCH PATTERNS

CABLE PATTERN 1

Row 1 (RS): P1, k8, p1.
Row 2: K1, p8, k1.
Row 3: P1, c4b, c4f, p1.
Row 4: K1, p2, k4, p2, k1.
Row 5: T3b, p4, t3f.
Row 6: P2, k6, p2.
Row 7: K2, p6, k2.
Row 8: As row 6.
Row 9: As row 7.
Row 10: As row 6.
Row 11: T3f, p4, t3b.
Row 12: As row 4.
Row 13: P1, c4f, c4b, p1.
Row 14: As row 2.
Row 15: As row 3.
Row 16: As row 2.
Row 17: As row 1.
Row 18: As row 2.
Row 19: As row 3.
Row 20: As row 2.
Repeat rows 1–20 for Cable Pattern 1.

CABLE PATTERN 2

Row 1: T3f, p4, t3b.
Row 2: K1, p8, k1.
Row 3: P1, c4f, c4b, p1.
Row 4: As row 2.
Row 5: P1, c4b, c4f, p1.
Row 6: As row 2.
Row 7: P1, k8, p1.
Row 8: As row 2.
Row 9: As row 5.
Row 10: As row 2.
Row 11: As row 7.
Row 12: As row 2.
Row 13: As row 5.
Row 14: K1, p2, k4, p2, k1.
Row 15: T3b, p4, t3f.
Row 16: P2, k6, p2.
Row 17: K2, p6, k2.
Row 18: As row 16.
Row 19: As row 17.
Row 20: As row 16.
Repeat rows 1–20 for Cable Pattern 2.

Sweater

Note The instructions are written for the smallest size. When changes are necessary for larger sizes, those instructions are enclosed in parentheses.

Back

**With smaller needles and MC, cast on 86 (98, 110, 122) stitches.

Row 1 K2, *p2, k2; repeat from * to end of row.

Row 2 P2, *k2, p2; repeat from * to end of row.

Repeat rows 1–2 until the Back measures 3" (7.5cm) from the cast-on edge, ending with RS facing for next row and increasing 16 (16, 14, 14) stitches evenly across the last row—102 (114, 124, 136) stitches.

Change to larger needles and proceed as follows:

Row 1 (RS) P2, [work row 1 of Cable Pattern 1, p1, work row 1 of Cable Pattern 2, p1] 4 (5, 5, 6) times, [work row 1 of Cable Pattern 1] 1 (0, 1, 0) time more, p2.

Row 2 K2, [work row 2 of Cable Pattern 1] 1 (0, 1, 0) time, [k1, work row 2 of Cable Pattern 2, k1, work row 2 of Cable Pattern 1] 4 (5, 5, 6) times, k2.

Cable Pattern is now set.

Continue in Cable Pattern until the Back measures 14 (14½, 15, 15½)" (35.5 [37, 38, 39.5]cm) from the cast-on edge, ending with RS facing for next row.

ARMHOLE SHAPING

Bind off 12 stitches at the beginning of the next 2 rows—78 (90, 100, 112) stitches.**

Continue in Cable Pattern until the armhole measures 9½ (10, 10½, 11)" (24 [25.5, 26.5, 28]cm), ending with RS facing for next row.

SHOULDER SHAPING

Bind off 7 (9, 10, 11) stitches at the beginning of the next 4 rows and then 7 (8, 9, 12) stitches at the beginning of the following 2 rows. Leave the remaining 36 (38, 42, 44) stitches on a stitch holder for the Back neck.

Front

Work from ** to ** as given for the Back.

Next Row (RS) Knit, decreasing 23 (23, 27, 31) stitches evenly across the row—55 (67, 73, 81) stitches.

Beginning with a purl row, work in stockinette stitch for 1½" (4.5cm), increasing 29 (23, 29, 33) stitches evenly across the last row—84 (90, 102, 114) stitches.

Work Chart, reading all right-side rows from right to left and all wrong-side rows from left to right.

Change to MC and purl 1 row, decreasing 29 (23, 29, 33) stitches evenly across the row. 55 (67, 73, 81) stitches. Beginning with a knit row, work in stockinette stitch for 1½" (4cm), increasing 23 (23, 27, 31) stitches evenly across last row—78 (90, 100, 112) stitches.

Next Row Work in Cable Pattern until the armhole measures 6 (6½, 7, 7½)" (15 [16.5, 18, 19]cm), ending with RS facing for next row.

NECK SHAPING (LEFT SIDE)

K33 (38, 43, 48). Place the remaining stitches on a holder. Turn. Maintaining Cable Pattern, decrease 1 stitch at the neck edge every row 12 (12, 14, 14) times, ending with RS facing for next row—21 (26, 29, 34) stitches.

Continue in Cable Pattern until the armhole measures 9½ (10, 10½, 11)" (24 [25.5, 26.5, 28]cm), ending with RS facing for next row.

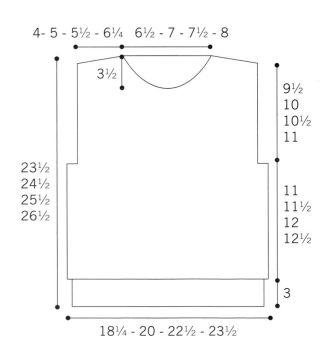

4- 5 - 5½ - 6¼   6½ - 7 - 7½ - 8

3½

9½
10
10½
11

23½
24½
25½
26½

11
11½
12
12½

3

18¼ - 20 - 22½ - 23½

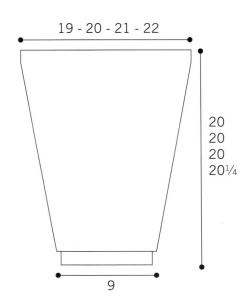

19 - 20 - 21 - 22

20
20
20
20¼

9

SHOULDER SHAPING (LEFT SIDE)

Bind off 7 (9, 10, 11) stitches at the beginning of the next 2 RS rows. Work 1 row even in pattern. Bind off the remaining stitches.

NECK SHAPING (RIGHT SIDE)

With RS facing, slip 12 (14, 14, 16) stitches from the stitch holder onto another stitch holder. Join the yarn and work in Cable Pattern, decreasing 1 stitch at the neck edge every row 12 (12, 14, 14) times—21 (26, 29, 34) stitches.

Continue in Cable Pattern until the armhole measures 9½ (10, 10½, 11)" (24 [25.5, 26.5, 28]cm), ending with WS facing for next row.

SHOULDER SHAPING (RIGHT SIDE)

Bind off 7 (9, 10, 11) stitches at the beginning of the next 2 WS rows. Work 1 row even in pattern. Bind off the remaining stitches.

Sleeves (Make 2)

With smaller needles and MC, cast on 50 stitches.

Row 1 K2, *p2, k2; repeat from * to end of row.

Row 2 P2, *k2, p2; repeat from * to end of row.

Repeat rows 1–2 until the Sleeve measures 3" (7.5cm) from the cast-on edge, ending with RS facing for next row, increasing 1 stitch at the center of the last row. 51 stitches.

Change to larger needles and proceed as follows:

Row 1 (RS) K2, p2, [work row 1 of Cable Pattern 1, p1, work row 1 of Cable Pattern 2, p1] 2 times, p1, k2.

Row 2 P2, k1, [k1, work row 2 of Cable Pattern 2, k1, work row 2 of Cable Pattern 1] 2 times, k2, p2.

Cable Pattern is now set.

Continue working Cable Pattern, AT THE SAME TIME increase 1 stitch at each end of the needle on the 3rd row and every 2nd row to 52 (54, 56, 56) stitches, then every 4th row to 104 (110, 116, 120) stitches, taking increased stitches into Cable Pattern. Work even until the Sleeve measures 20 (20, 20, 20¼)" (51 [51, 51, 51.5]cm) from the cast-on edge. Bind off.

6 st repeat

KEY

☐ = MC

● = A

— = B

Finishing

Block the pieces to the measurements.

With B, embroider on the Front as pictured.

Sew the left shoulder seam.

NECK BAND

With smaller needles and RS facing, with MC pick up and knit 17 stitches down the left Front neck. Knit across 12 (14, 14, 16) stitches on the stitch holder. Pick up and knit 17 stitches up the right Front neck. Knit across 36 (38, 42, 44) stitches on the Back neck stitch holder. 82 (86, 90, 94) stitches. Work in k2, p2 ribbing as given for the Back for 4" (10cm). Bind off in ribbing.

Sew the right shoulder and the neckband seam. Sew in the Sleeves. Sew the sleeve and side seams.

LEAF STITCH

FRENCH KNOT

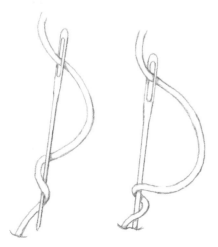

Fair Isle

Fair Isle is a technique that creates a pattern by changing two or more colors within a row. When changing colors for Fair Isle mid-row, always bring the yarn you need from beneath the "live" (or active) yarn. Every 3 to 4 stitches, the yarn not in use should be woven into the work:

Place the inactive yarn (to be woven) over the tip of the left-hand needle. Knit the next stitch as you would normally, being careful not to knit the woven yarn. Rather, let it be caught and secured.

It is important not to work in Fair Isle too tightly or too loosely. Practice on a swatch before working on the sweater.

Twist yarn at the ends of rows to carry the yarn along the sides. That way, there are fewer ends to sew in when you are finished knitting.

Hat

**With smaller double-pointed needles and MC, cast on 112 stitches. Divide stitches evenly on 3 needles (37, 38, 37 stitches each). Join to work in the round. Place marker.

Rnd 1 *K2, p2; repeat from * to end of round.

Repeat round 1 of ribbing until the Hat measures 1½" (4cm) from the cast-on edge, increasing 2 stitches evenly on the last round. 114 stitches. Change to larger double-pointed needles and begin Chart A, reading rounds from right to left on every round. Work to end of chart.

Next Rnd With MC, knit 1 round, decreasing 34 stitches evenly across—80 stitches.

Work in stockinette stitch until Hat measures 6" (15cm) from the cast-on edge.

Next Rnd *K6, k2tog; repeat from * to end of round. 70 stitches.

Next Rnd Knit.

Next Rnd *K5, k2tog; repeat from * to end of round. 60 stitches.

Continue decreasing 10 stitches as established every other round until there are 20 stitches.

Next Rnd Knit.

Next Rnd *K2tog; repeat from * to end of round. 10 stitches.

Next Rnd *K2tog; repeat from * to end of round. 5 stitches. Break the yarn and thread through remaining stitches. Pull tight, and fasten.

With B, embroider on the Hat as pictured.

TASSEL (MAKE 1)

Wind MC 30 times around one hand. Break the yarn, leaving a long end. Thread through a tapestry needle. Slip the needle through the loops and tie tightly. Wind the yarn 5 times around, 1" (2.5cm) below one fold. Secure. Cut through the end of the loops and trim evenly. Cut an 18" (45.75cm) strand of MC. Fold the strand in half and twist until it curls onto itself and twists in half. Attach the twisted strand to the Tassel and to the top of the Hat.

FEBRUARY

I COME FROM A LARGE FAMILY. When I began Baa Baa Knits (a company I started in the 1990s for selling my designs in kit form), I recruited models I could afford—who would work for love or for wool and sweaters. Naturally, this began with my family and friends. When I found a few takers, I packed up my samples and camera and we headed to a local park by a lake. One thing I had learned from my days at the Patons design studio was that outdoor shots look best—especially if you have a waterfront location.

I have no formal photography training, so we laughed hard and loud as I positioned the models and they posed for me. Overall, the shots came out great. I asked my nephew, Scott, to pose for this book, along with other family members and friends. The photos for the Boyfriend Sweater (page 34), shot at the crack of dawn, were taken with Scott's girlfriend, Deb, nearby, so it wasn't difficult for him to look the part.

Think of love when knitting the Boyfriend Sweater. Or dream of romance while clicking away at the Kiss Curls Snuggle Wrap (page 30), and remember your little Valentine while sewing up the Girl's Valentine Cardie (page 27).

27

30

34

Let me not to the marriage of true minds Admit impediments: love is not love Which alters when it alteration finds.
—WILLIAM SHAKESPEARE (1564–1616), "SONNET 116"

Girl's Valentine Cardie

This is one a child will love to wear. The yarn is soft and comfortable with a little something to jazz it up. Emma, our little model, wanted to wear it home. How could I not let her?

Beginner

SIZE

Age: 2 (4, 6, 8, 10) years

Chest measurement: 21 (23, 25, 26½, 28)" (53.5 [58.5, 63.5, 67.5, 71]cm)

Finished chest: 24 (26, 29, 31½, 31½)" (61 [66, 74, 80, 80]cm)

MATERIALS

6 (7, 8, 9, 11) balls Needful Yarns King Stampato Extra (1¾ oz [50g]/99 yds [90.5m]; 100% merino wool), #8022 Pink, (4) medium

1 pair US 7 (4.5mm) needles

1 pair US 8 (5mm) needles or size required to achieve gauge

1 stitch holder

GAUGE

19 stitches and 20 rows = 4" (10cm) in stockinette stitch with larger needles

STITCH PATTERN

PATTERN STITCH

Row 1 (RS): K3, *p3, k3; repeat from * to end of row.
Row 2: P3, *k3, p3; repeat from * to end of row.
Rows 3–4: Repeat rows 1–2.
Row 5: As for row 2.
Row 6: As for row 1.
Rows 7–8: Repeat rows 5–6.
Repeat rows 1–8 for the Pattern Stitch.

Note The instructions are written for the smallest size. When changes are necessary for larger sizes, those instructions are enclosed in parentheses.

Back

With smaller needles, cast on 90 (101, 112, 112, 123) stitches.

EDGING

Row 1 (WS) Purl.

Row 2 K2, *k1, slip this stitch back to left-hand needle, pass the next 8 stitches on left-hand needle over the first one, yo twice, knit this stitch again, k2; repeat from * to end.

Row 3 K1, *p2tog, work (k1, p1, k1, p1, k1) into double yo (dropping 2nd yo) of the previous row, p1; repeat from * to last stitch, k1—58 (65, 72, 72, 79) stitches.

Knit 3 rows, decrease 1 (decrease 2, decrease 3, increase 3, decrease 4) stitches evenly across the last row—57 (63, 69, 75, 75) stitches.

BODY

Next Row (RS) K1, *p1, k1; repeat from * to end of row.

Repeat this row for seed stitch for 1½" (4cm), ending with WS facing for next row.

Next Row Purl.

Change to larger needles and work in Pattern Stitch until the Back measures 5¾ (6, 6½, 8, 9½)" (14.5 [15, 16.5, 20.5, 24]cm) from seed stitch, ending with RS facing for next row.

ARMHOLE SHAPING

Bind off 6 stitches at the beginning of the next 2 rows—45 (51, 57, 63, 63) stitches.

Continue even in pattern until the Back measures 11¼ (12¼, 13¼, 15¼, 16¾)" (31 [33.5, 38.5, 42.5]cm) from the cast-on edge, ending with RS facing for next row.

SHOULDER SHAPING

Bind off 4 (5, 7, 8, 8) stitches at the beginning of the next 2 rows, then 5 (6, 7, 8, 8) stitches at the beginning of the next 2 rows. Leave the remaining 27 (29, 29, 31, 31) stitches on a stitch holder.

Left Front

**With smaller needles, cast on 46 (46, 46, 57, 57) stitches.

Work 3 rows of Edging as given for the Back to 30 (30, 30, 37, 37) stitches. Knit 3 rows, decreasing 3 (increasing 3, increasing 3, increasing 2, increasing 2) stitches evenly across the last row—27 (33, 33, 39, 39) stitches.

Work in seed stitch as given for the Back for 1½" (4cm), ending with facing for next row.

Next row Purl.

Change to larger needles and work in Pattern Stitch until the Left Front measures 5¾ (6, 6½, 8, 9½)" (14.5 [15, 16.5, 20.5, 24]cm) from seed stitch, ending with RS facing for next row.

ARMHOLE SHAPING

Bind off 6 stitches at the beginning of the next row—21 (27, 27, 33, 33) stitches.

Continue even in Pattern Stitch until the Left Front measures 9¼ (10, 10½, 12½, 13½)" (23.5 [25.5, 26.5, 32, 34.5]cm) from the cast-on edge, ending with WS facing for next row.

NECK SHAPING

Bind off 4 (5, 5, 5, 5) stitches, work in Pattern Stitch to end.

Decrease 1 stitch at the neck edge on next and every 2nd row to 9 (11, 14, 16, 16) stitches.

Continue even in Pattern Stitch until the Left Front measures the same length as the Back before shoulder shaping, ending with RS facing for next row.

SHOULDER SHAPING

Bind off 4 (5, 7, 8, 8) stitches at the beginning of the next row. Work 1 row even. Bind off the remaining stitches.

Right Front

Work from ** to ** as given for the Left Front.

Change to larger needles and work in Pattern Stitch until the Right Front measures 5¾ (6, 6½, 8, 9½)" (14.5 [15, 16.5, 20.5, 24]cm) from seed stitch, ending with WS facing for next row.

ARMHOLE SHAPING

Bind off 6 stitches at the beginning of the next row—21 (27, 27, 33, 33) stitches.

Continue even in Pattern Stitch until the Right Front measures 9¼ (10, 10½, 12½, 13½)" (23 [25.5, 26.5, 32, 34.5]cm) from the cast-on edge, ending with RS facing for next row.

NECK SHAPING

Bind off 4 (5, 5, 5, 5) stitches, work in Pattern Stitch to end.

Decrease 1 stitch at the neck edge on next and every 2nd row to 9 (11, 14, 16, 16) stitches.

Continue even in Pattern Stitch until the Right Front measures the same length as the Back before shoulder shaping, with WS facing for next row.

SHOULDER SHAPING

Bind off 4 (5, 7, 8, 8) stitches at the beginning of the next row. Work 1 row even. Bind off the remaining stitches.

Sleeves (Make 2)

With smaller needles, cast on 46 (46, 57, 57, 57) stitches.

Work 3 rows of Edging as given for the Back—30 (30, 37, 37, 37) stitches.

Knit 3 rows, increasing 3 stitches across last row—33 (33, 40, 40, 40) stitches.

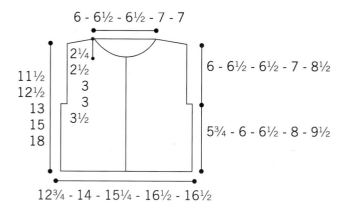

6 - 6½ - 6½ - 7 - 7

2¼
2½
3
3
3½

11½
12½
13
15
18

6 - 6½ - 6½ - 7 - 8½

5¾ - 6 - 6½ - 8 - 9½

12¾ - 14 - 15¼ - 16½ - 16½

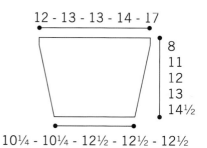

12 - 13 - 13 - 14 - 17

8
11
12
13
14½

10¼ - 10¼ - 12½ - 12½ - 12½

Work in seed stitch as given for Back for 1¼" (3cm), ending with RS facing for next row—33 (33, 40, 40, 40) stitches.

Change to larger needles and work in Pattern Stitch, increasing 1 stitch at each end of the needle on the 3rd row and following 2nd row to 55 (51, 44, 48, 64) stitches, then every following 4th row to 57 (61, 62, 68, 80) stitches.

Continue in Pattern Stitch until the Sleeve measures 8 (11, 12, 13, 14½)" (20.5 [28, 30.5, 37]cm) from the cast-on edge, ending with RS facing for next row. Bind off all stitches.

Finishing

Pin all pieces to measurements and cover with a damp cloth. Leave the cloth to dry on the garment.

Sew the shoulder seams.

BUTTONHOLE BAND

With RS facing and smaller needles, pick up and knit 55 (63, 67, 75, 83) stitches up Right Front edge.

Work 3 rows in seed stitch.

Row 4 (RS) Work 2 stitches in seed stitch, *bind off 2 (buttonhole made), work in seed stitch 10 (12, 13, 15, 17) stitches; repeat from * 3 more times, bind off 2, work 3 stitches in seed stitch.

Row 5 Work in seed stitch, casting on 2 stitches over the bound-off stitches.

Work 2 more rows in seed stitch. Bind off all stitches.

BUTTON BAND

Work as for Buttonhole Band, omitting the buttonholes.

COLLAR

With smaller needles, cast on 90 (101, 101, 101, 101) stitches. Work Edging as given for Back to 58 (65, 65, 65, 65) stitches. Knit 3 rows, increasing 0 (decreasing 3, increasing 1, increasing 3, increasing 3) evenly across the last row. 58 (62, 66, 68, 68) stitches. Work in seed stitch for 1½" (4cm). Bind off all stitches in seed stitch.

Sew the Collar to the neck edge, beginning at the halfway point of the Button Bands.

Sew in the Sleeves. Sew the side and Sleeve seams. Sew on the buttons, matching them to the buttonholes.

Edgings

Edgings can be interchangeable. To re-create the Girl's Valentine Cardie with a different look, choose a different edging from a stitch dictionary (one from the Harmony Guides or Barbara Walker's books would be a good start) that is worked vertically (rather than sideways). Do a swatch of about 4" (10cm). You will have to cast on enough stitches to get as close to the width as possible while working within the multiple of stitches required for your chosen edging. Work the edging, and then purl a row on the wrong side and decrease or increase enough stitches to get to 57 stitches (for size Small, Back)—where this pattern picks up after the edging.

Kiss Curls Snuggle Wrap

This one is for the gals from the Ottawa Knitting Guild. During a design class I gave there, the women took notice of the wrap I was wearing. I had to take it off while we "dissected" it. We took measurements and considered ways to improve on the design. I made it more casual and "unconstructed," omitting edgings and bands. From there, I was curious to see how it would look in different yarn. I fell in love with this Fleece Artist Kiss Curls yarn (along with the whole line of Fleece Artist). The result is a useful, great-looking garment that can go dressy or casual.

Intermediate

SIZE

Small (Medium, Large)

Bust: 30–32 (34–36, 38–40)"
(76–81.5 [86.5–91.5,
96.5–101.5]cm)

Finished size: 32 (36, 40)"
(78.5 [88, 98]cm)

MATERIALS

1 (1, 2) hanks Fleece Artist Kiss
Curls (8¾ [250g]/1,093 yds
[1,000m]; 86% kid/14%
nylon), Burgundy, (**4**) medium

1 pair US 10.5 (6.5mm)
straight needles or size needed
to obtain gauge

GAUGE

16 stitches and 22 rows = 4"
(10cm) in stockinette stitch

Note The instructions are written for the smallest size. When changes are necessary for larger sizes, those instructions are enclosed in parentheses.

Back

Cast on 64 (72, 80) stitches.

Knit 1 row.

Beginning with a knit row, work in stockinette stitch until the Back measures 8½ (9, 9½)" (21.5 [23, 24]cm) from the cast-on edge, ending with RS facing for next row.

ARMHOLE SHAPING

Bind off 3 stitches at the beginning of the next 2 rows—58 (66, 74) stitches.

Decrease 1 stitch at each end of the needle on the next 3

(5, 6) alternate rows. 52 (56, 62) stitches.

Continue even in stockinette stitch until the armhole measures 7½ (8, 8½)" (19 [20.5, 21.5]cm), ending with RS facing for next row.

SHOULDER SHAPING

Bind off 5 (5, 6) stitches at the beginning of the next 4 rows, then 4 (5, 5) stitches at the beginning of the following 2 rows. Bind off remaining 24 (26, 28) stitches.

Left Front

Cast on 48 (52, 56) stitches.

Knit 1 row.

Beginning with a knit row, work 5 rows in stockinette stitch.

Row 6 (WS) Bind off 20 stitches, purl to end—28 (32, 36) stitches.

Row 7 Knit to last 2 stitches, k2tog—27 (31, 35) stitches.

Rows 8–17 Work in stockinette stitch.

Repeat rows 7–17 until the Left Front is the same length as the Back to the armhole shaping, ending with RS facing for next row.

ARMHOLE SHAPING

Bind off 3 stitches, knit to last 2 stitches, k2tog.

Next Row Purl.

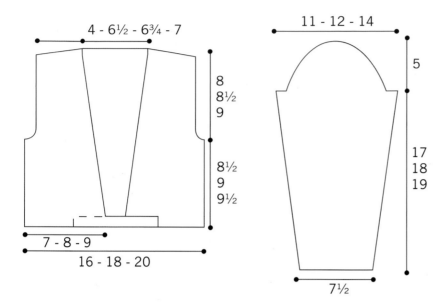

Decrease 1 stitch at the armhole edge on the next 3 (5, 6) alternate rows, AT THE SAME TIME decrease 1 stitch at the neck edge every 10th row until there are 16 (16, 17) stitches remaining. Work even in stockinette stitch until the armhole measures 7½ (8, 8½)" (19 [20.5, 21.5]cm), ending with RS facing for next row.

SHOULDER SHAPING

Bind off 5 (5, 6) stitches at the beginning of the next 2 alternate rows. Work 1 row even. Bind off the remaining stitches.

Right Front

Cast on 48 (52, 56) stitches.

Knit 1 row.

Beginning with a knit row, work 4 rows in stockinette stitch.

Row 5 (RS) Bind off 20 stitches, knit to end—28 (32, 36) stitches.

Row 6 Purl to last 2 stitches, p2tog. 27 (31, 35) stitches.

Rows 7–16 Work in stockinette stitch.

Repeat rows 6–16 until the Right Front is the same length as the Back to the armhole shaping, ending with WS facing for next row.

ARMHOLE SHAPING

Bind off 3 stitches, purl to last 2 stitches, p2tog.

Decrease 1 stitch at the armhole edge on the next 3 (5, 6) alternate rows, AT THE SAME TIME decrease 1 stitch at the neck edge every 10th row until there are 16 (16, 17) stitches remaining. Work even in stockinette stitch until the armhole measures 7½ (8, 8½)" (19 [20.5, 21.5]cm), ending with WS facing for next row.

SHOULDER SHAPING

Bind off 5 (5, 6) stitches at the beginning of the next 2 alternate rows. Work 1 row even. Bind off the remaining stitches.

Sleeves (Make 2)

Cast on 30 stitches. Knit 1 row. Beginning with a knit row, work in stockinette stitch, increasing 1 stitch at each end of the needle on the 3rd and following 12th (10th, 6th) rows 2 (3, 2) times, then every 14th (12th, 8th) row until there are 44 (48, 56) stitches.

Continue in stockinette stitch until the Sleeves measure 17 (18, 19)" (43 [45.5, 48]cm) from the cast-on edge, ending with RS facing for next row.

SHAPE CAP

Bind off 2 (3, 3) stitches at the beginning of the next 2 (2, 3) rows, then 2 stitches at the beginning of the following 2 rows—36 (38, 44) stitches

Decrease 1 stitch at each end of the needle every 4th row 4 (3, 0) times, then every following alternate row 0 (2, 8) times—28 stitches.

Bind off 2 stitches at the beginning of the next 6 rows—16 stitches.

Bind off all stitches.

Finishing

Block the pieces to the measurements. Sew the shoulder seams. Sew in the Sleeves. Sew the side and Sleeve seams.

Blocking

Once your pieces are knit up, you need to block them to size (unless the instructions advise differently). There are two typical ways you can do this—and then there is my method, which is a form of steam blocking. The two more common methods are to wet block and to steam block. To wet block, you soak your knitting in cold water, loosely roll it in a towel, and then pin to the measurements. This is not my favorite method, because handling any wool while wet is asking for trouble, but it is good for cabled work or ribbing. To steam block, you pin the work to the measurements first, then place a damp towel over the piece and press lightly with an iron, without moving the iron around very much.

For my method, I pin the pieces to the measurements given in the schematics. Then, with my iron set on steam, I hover the iron over the work to gently moisten it. Once the piece is thoroughly moistened, I place a towel over it and leave the work to dry. The towel prevents curling and absorbs moisture. Never press your knitting directly; it destroys your time-invested hard work!

Boyfriend Sweater

We still do it—we fall in love and then feel the overwhelming need to make something for the object of our affection to let him know how special he makes us feel. It helps if it doesn't have a reindeer on it (à la Bridget Jones's Diary). You want the person to wear it and feel loved.

SKILL LEVEL
Experienced

SIZE
Small (Medium, Large, X-Large)

Chest size: 36 (43½, 47, 52½)" (91.5 [110.5, 119.5, 133.5]cm)

MATERIALS
Tahki Donegal Tweed (1¾ oz [50g]/183 yds [167m]; 100% pure new wool) (4) medium
2 (2, 3, 4) hanks #845 Purple (MC)

2 hanks #848 Oatmeal (A)
2 hanks #805 Navy (B)
2 hanks #894 Forest (C)

1 pair US 7 (4.5mm) needles

1 pair US 8 (5mm) needles or size required to achieve gauge

3 stitch holders

GAUGE
18 stitches and 24 rows = 4" (10cm) in reverse stockinette stitch with larger needles

Note The instructions are written for the smallest size. When changes are necessary for larger sizes, those instructions are enclosed in parentheses.

Back

**With smaller needles and MC, cast on 82 (98, 106, 118) stitches.

Row 1 K2, *p2, k2; repeat from * to end of row.

Row 2 P2, *k2, p2; repeat from * to end of row.

Repeat rows 1–2 until the Back measures 3" (7.5cm) from the cast-on edge, ending with RS facing for next row.

Change to larger needles and work in reverse stockinette stitch (purl on the right-side rows and knit on the wrong-side rows) until the Back measures 15½ (16, 16¼, 16½)" (39.5 [40.5, 41.5, 42]cm) from the cast-on edge, ending with RS facing for next row.

ARMHOLE SHAPING

Next Row Bind off 4 stitches, p0 (0, 7, 7), *p2 (3, 2, 5), Inc1P; repeat from * to last 6 (6, 11, 11) stitches, p6 (6, 11, 11)—102 (116, 130, 130) stitches.

Next Row Bind off 4 stitches, knit to end of row—98 (112, 126, 126) stitches.**

Work Chart, noting that the 28-stitch repeat is worked 3 (4, 4, 4) times, then the first 14 stitches 1 (0, 1, 1) time more, until the armhole measures 9½ (10, 10½, 11)" (24 [25.5, 26.5, 28]cm), ending with RS facing for next row.

SHOULDER SHAPING

Bind off 9 (11, 13, 13) stitches at the beginning of the next 4 rows, then 8 (11, 13, 13) stitches at the beginning of the following 2 rows. Leave the remaining 46 (46, 48, 48) stitches on a stitch holder for the back neck.

Front

Work from ** to ** as for the Back.

Work Chart, noting that the 28-stitch repeat is worked 3 (4, 4, 4) times, then the first 14 stitches 1 (0, 1, 1) time more, until the armhole measures 6 (6½, 7, 7½)" (15 [16.5, 18, 19]cm), ending with RS facing for next row.

NECK SHAPING (LEFT SIDE)

Next Row Work in pattern for 37 (44, 51, 51) stitches, turn. Leave the remaining stitches on a stitch holder.

Continuing with the Chart, decrease 1 stitch at the neck edge on the next 4 (4, 6, 6) rows, then every 2nd row until there are 26 (33, 39, 39) stitches remaining.

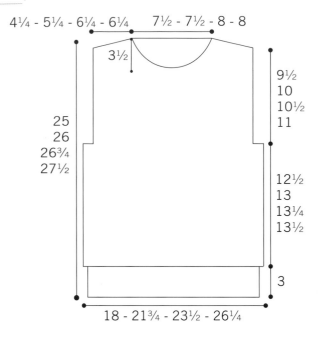

4¼ - 5¼ - 6¼ - 6¼   7½ - 7½ - 8 - 8

3½

25
26
26¾
27½

9½
10
10½
11

12½
13
13¼
13½

3

18 - 21¾ - 23½ - 26¼

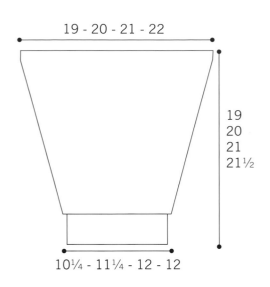

19 - 20 - 21 - 22

19
20
21
21½

10¼ - 11¼ - 12 - 12

Work even in Chart until the armhole measures 9½ (10, 10½, 11)" (24 [25.5, 26.5, 28]cm), ending with RS facing for next row.

SHOULDER SHAPING (LEFT SIDE)

Bind off 9 (11, 13, 13) stitches at the beginning of the next and following alternate row. Bind off the remaining 8 (11, 13, 13) stitches.

NECK SHAPING (RIGHT SIDE)

With RS facing, slip 24 stitches from the stitch holder onto another stitch holder. Join the yarn to the remaining stitches and work in pattern to end.

Continuing with Chart, decrease 1 stitch at the neck edge on the next 4 (4, 6, 6) rows, then every 2nd row until there are 26 (33, 39, 39) stitches remaining.

Joining New Yarn

When changing colors at the end of a row, tie the new color of yarn to the old one. Don't forget to untie the knot when you're finished, so you can weave in the ends with a tapestry needle. Alternatively, you can weave the yarn ends into the knitting, along the old color row, by using the same method used in Fair Isle knitting (see page 120).

Work even in Chart until the armhole measures 9½ (10, 10½, 11)" (24 [25.5, 26.5, 28]cm), ending with WS facing for next row.

SHOULDER SHAPING (RIGHT SIDE)

Bind off 9 (11, 13, 13) stitches at the beginning of the next and following alternate row. Bind off the remaining 8 (11, 13, 13) stitches.

Sleeves (Make 2)

With smaller needles and MC, cast on 46 (50, 54, 54) stitches.

Row 1 K2, *p2, k2; repeat from * to end of row.

Row 2 P2, *k2, p2; repeat from * to end of row.

Repeat rows 1–2 until the Sleeve measures 3" (7.5cm) from the cast-on edge, ending with RS facing for next row.

Change to larger needles and work in reverse stockinette stitch, increasing 1 stitch at each end of the needle on the 3rd and every following 4th row to 76 (76, 78, 82) stitches, then every 6th row to 86 (90, 94, 98) stitches.

Continue even until the Sleeve measures 19 (20, 21, 21½)" (48 [51, 53.5, 54.5]cm) from the cast-on edge. Place markers at each end of the last row.

Work 6 rows even. Bind off all stitches.

Finishing

Block all the pieces to the measurements. Sew the left shoulder seam.

NECKBAND

With smaller needles and MC, and with RS facing, pick up and knit 16 stitches down the left Front neck. Knit 24 stitches from the stitch holder. Pick up and knit 16 stitches up the right Front neck. Knit 46 (46, 48, 48) stitches from the Back neck stitch holder, decreasing 0 (0, 2, 2) stitches evenly across—102 stitches.

Starting with row 2, work in (k2, p2) ribbing as for the Back for 4" (10cm), ending with RS facing for next row. Bind off in ribbing.

Sew the right shoulder seam. Fold the neckband over to the inside and stitch into place.

Sew in the Sleeves, placing the rows above the markers along the bind-off stitches at the Front and Back to form square armholes. Sew the Sleeve and side seams.

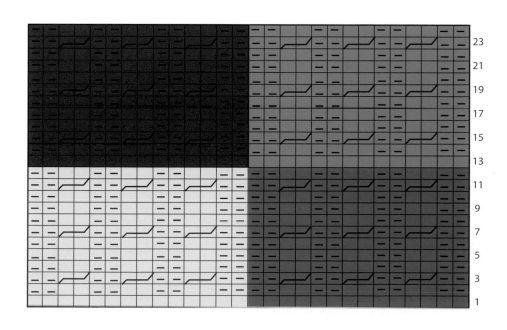

 = Knit on RS/Purl on WS

 = Purl on RS/Knit on WS

= C2R (cable 2 right)

MARCH

The knitting book that has inspired me the most in my time as a designer was Nicky Epstein's *Knitted Embellishments*, which came out in 1999. For me, it was the best thing that came out in knitting that year. After I got my hands on a copy, most of my designs for that year were influenced by and adorned with ideas from her book. Embellishment became my passion and it still lives on today.

Almost any garment can go from ho-hum to zing with a little adornment. While the Holiday Beach Cover-Up (page 46) can be simplified by leaving the appliqués off, I love the kitschy-ness they bring to the design. (If I could have found some tacky earrings for Sarah, the model, during this shoot, she'd be wearing them!) These appliqués can embellish almost anything.

*To live a creative life—
we must lose our fear
of being wrong.*
—JOSEPH CHILTON PEARCE

Key West Crop Top

This little number is a beginner pattern with a twist. If you feel confident, I have added a little challenge: the holes. Try it and see how you do. If you want, you can ignore the holes and continue in stockinette stitch, making an equally attractive top.

Beginner

SIZE
Small (Medium, Large, X-Large)

Bust: 30–32 (34–36, 38–40, 42–44)" (76–81.5 [86.5–91.5, 96.5–101.5, 106.5–112]cm)

Finished size: 34 (37, 40, 43)" (86.25 [94, 101.5, 109]cm)

MATERIALS
4 (4, 4, 5) hanks Rowan Summer Tweed (1¾ oz [50g]/118 yds [108m]; 30% silk/70% cotton), #512 Exotic, **4** medium

1 pair US 7 (4.5mm) needles

1 pair US 8 (5mm) needles or size required to achieve gauge

2 stitch holders

GAUGE
16 stitches and 23 rows= 4" (10cm) in stockinette stitch with larger needles

Note The instructions are written for the smallest size. When changes are necessary for larger sizes, those instructions are enclosed in parentheses.

Back

**With smaller needles, cast on 68 (74, 80, 86) stitches.

Row 1 (RS) *K1, p1; repeat from * to end of row.

Row 2 *P1, k1; repeat from * to end of row.

Repeat rows 1–2 for seed stitch for 1" (2.5cm), ending with RS facing for next row.

Change to larger needles and work in stockinette stitch for 1" (2.5cm), ending with RS facing for next row.

FIRST SECTION OF HOLE PATTERN
Row 1 (RS) K4 (7, 8, 9), k2tog, turn, place remaining stitches on a spare needle, turn.

Row 2 and All WS Rows Purl.

Row 3 K3 (6, 7, 8), k2tog, turn.

Row 5 K2 (5, 6, 7), k2tog, turn.

Row 7 K1 (4, 5, 6), k2tog, turn.

Row 9 K1 (4, 5, 6), k1f&b, turn.

Row 11 K2 (5, 6, 7), k1f&b, turn.

Row 13 K3 (6, 7, 8), k1f&b, turn.

Row 15 K4 (7, 8, 9), k1f&b. Place these stitches on a spare needle. Break the yarn.

HOLE SPACING
Row 1 (RS) Join yarn to spare needle stitches, k2tog, k10 (10, 11, 12), k2tog, turn, place remaining stitches on a spare needle, turn.

Row 2 and All WS Rows Purl.

Row 3 K2tog, k8 (8, 9, 10), k2tog, turn.

Row 5 K2tog, k6 (6, 7, 8), k2tog, turn.

Row 7 K2tog, k4 (4, 5, 6), k2tog, turn.

Row 9 K1, m1, k4 (4, 5, 6), k1f&b, turn.

Row 11 K1, m1, k6 (6, 7, 8), k1f&b, turn.

Row 13 K1, m1, k8 (8, 9, 10), k1f&b, turn.

Row 15 K1, m1, k10 (10, 11, 12), knit to end. Place these stitches on a spare needle. Break the yarn.

Repeat rows 1–15 three times. Four holes made.

LAST CORNER
Row 1 (RS) Join yarn to remaining stitches, k2tog, knit to end.

Row 2 Purl.

Repeat rows 1–2 three more times.

Row 9 K1, m1, knit to end.

Row 10 Purl.

Repeat rows 9–10 three more times.

Five holes made.

BACK CONTINUED

Work in stockinette stitch across all stitches until the Back measures 7½ (8, 8½, 9)" (19 [20.5, 21.5, 23]cm) from the cast-on edge, ending with RS facing for next row. If you chose not to make the holes, work in stockinette stitch to given measurement.

ARMHOLE SHAPING

Bind off 2 stitches at the beginning of the next 2 rows—64 (70, 76, 82) stitches.**

Continuing in stockinette stitch, decrease 1 stitch at each end of the needle every RS row 7 (11, 16, 21) times. Then decrease 1 stitch at each end of the needle every 4th row 7 (6, 4, 2) times—36 stitches.

Continue even in stockinette stitch until the armhole measures 7½ (8, 8½, 9)" (19 [20.5, 21.5, 23]cm), ending with RS facing for next row. Place all stitches on a stitch holder for back neck.

Front

Work from ** to ** as for the Back.

ARMHOLE SHAPING

Work armhole decreases as given for the Back until there are 46 (50, 52, 54) stitches and the armhole measures approximately 6 (6½, 7, 7½)" (15 [16.5, 18, 19]cm), ending with RS facing for next row.

NECK SHAPING (LEFT SIDE)

Next Row K17 (19, 20, 21) stitches, turn. Place remaining stitches on spare needle.

Next Row Purl.

Continuing in stockinette stitch, decrease 1 stitch at the neck edge every row 6 times, then every alternate row 6 times. Bind off.

NECK SHAPING (RIGHT SIDE)

With RS facing, place the next 12 stitches from the spare needle on a stitch holder for the Front neck. Decrease 1 stitch at the neck edge every row 6 times, then every alternate row 6 times. Bind off.

Finishing

Block the pieces to the measurements. Sew the right shoulder seam.

COLLAR

With RS facing, pick up and knit 14 stitches down the left front neck. Knit across the 12 stitches on the stitch holder. Pick up and knit 14 stitches up the right Front neck. Knit across the 36 stitches on the Back neck stitch holder. 76 stitches. Work in seed stitch as given for the Back for 2½" (6cm). Bind off in seed stitch.

ARMBANDS

With RS facing, pick up and knit 30 stitches around the armholes. Bind off all stitches.

Sew the left shoulder seam and the side seams.

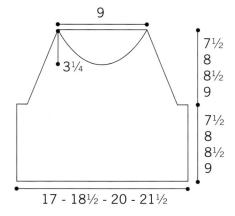

9

7½
8
8½
9

3¼

7½
8
8½
9

17 - 18½ - 20 - 21½

BVI Bikini

This bikini is for those who know (or aren't afraid to learn) how to crochet. The bikini is knit first and then edged with crochet.

Intermediate

SIZE
To fit A (B, C) cup bust

Bottom: One size

MATERIALS
1 skein SR Kertzer Butterfly Super 10 (4½ oz [125g]/250 yds [228m]; 100% mercerized cotton), #3401 Orange, **3** light

1 pair US 7 (4.5mm) needles or size required to achieve gauge

1 US G-6 (4mm) crochet hook

Clear elastic knitting thread

5" (12.5cm) square swimsuit lining (optional)

GAUGE
20 stitches and 26 rows = 4" (10cm) in stockinette stitch

Note The instructions are written for the smallest size. When changes are necessary for larger sizes, those instructions are enclosed in parentheses.

Top

CUP (MAKE 2)
Cast on 29 (33, 37) stitches.

Row 1 (RS) Knit.

Row 2 Purl.

Row 3 K1, sl1, k1, psso, knit to last 3 stitches, k2tog, k1.

Row 4 Purl.

Row 5 Knit.

Row 6 Purl.

Repeat rows 3–6 until there are 19 stitches remaining.

**Next Row K1, sl1, k1, psso, *yo, k2tog; repeat from * to last 2 stitches, k2tog—17 stitches.

Next Row Purl. **

Repeat from ** to ** until there are 5 stitches remaining.

Next Row (RS) K1, sl1, k2tog, psso, k1—3 stitches.

Next Row P3tog, sl remaining st (top of cup) onto crochet hook, ch 3, work 20 (24, 28) hdc down first side edge, ch 3 at corner, work 21 (25, 29) hdc across bottom edge, ch 3 at corner, work 20 (24, 28) hdc up second side edge, sl st to 2nd ch of first ch 3, fasten off.

STRAPS

With crochet hook, join yarn with sl st to top corner ch-1 space of first Cup. Make a chain 15½" (39.5cm) long. Fasten off. Repeat for second Cup.

With RS facing, join yarn with sl st to ch-3 space at bottom right-hand corner of first cup, then (ch 3, hdc) in same space, hdc in each st along bottom edge to left-hand corner, ch 5, hdc in ch-3 space at bottom right-hand corner of second cup, then hdc in each st along bottom edge of second cup to last st, 2 hdc in ch 3 sp at bottom left-hand corner of second cup, ch 3, turn.

Row 2 Work 2 hdc in first ch 3 sp, hdc in each st to last st, 2 hdc in last ch 3 sp, ch 3, turn.

Row 3 Work 2 hdc in first ch 3 sp, hdc in each st to last st, 2 hdc in last ch 3 sp, then work chain st to create strap 20½" (52cm) long, fasten off.

Sl st to first st on outside corner of remaining cup, then work same-length strap in same manner.

Bottom

Cast on 41 stitches.

Row 1 (RS) K1, sl1, k1, psso, *yo, k2tog; repeat from * to last 2 stitches, k2tog—39 stitches.

Row 2 Purl.

Repeat rows 1–2 four times more—31 stitches.

Begin working in stockinette stitch, continuing to decrease 1 stitch at each end of the needle as in row 1 on the next and every alternate row until there are 15 stitches remaining.

Work even in stockinette stitch for 5" (12.5cm), ending with RS facing for next row.

Increase 1 stitch at each end of the needle on every row until there are 61 stitches. Work even in stockinette stitch until the Bottom measures 17½" (44.5cm) from the cast-on edge, ending with RS facing for next row. Bind off, leaving the last stitch on the needle.

Slip the remaining stitch onto the crochet hook. Ch 3, work 62 hdc along the first side edge, ch 3 at corner, work 31 hdc across the top front edge, ch 3 at corner, work 62 hdc along second side edge, ch 3 at corner, work 40 hdc across the top back edge, sl st to 2nd ch of first ch 3, work chain st 15½" (39.5cm) long for Strap. Fasten off.

Sl st to next corner ch-3 sp of front. Make a chain 15½" (39.5cm) long for strap. Fasten off.

Repeat for 2 remaining corners.

Finishing

Sew elastic thread along each side of the leg openings and around each bra cup. Optional: Sew swimsuit lining into crotch using a ¼" (6mm) seam allowance.

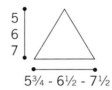

Crochet

By mastering the crochet chain, you can make nice, skinny straps for your knitting. Learning the basics of crochet can add to a knitter's cache of options—for example, the hdc can simply be changed to sc or dc for another look.

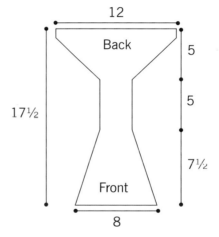

5
6
7

5¾ - 6½ - 7½

12

Back

5

17½

5

7½

Front

8

Holiday Beach Cover-Up

This cover-up is airy enough not to be heavy, yet absorbs moisture like a towel.
Any color will coordinate well, making it a timeless piece.

Experienced

SIZE
Small (Medium, Large, X-Large)

Bust: 30–32 (34–36, 38–40, 42–44)" (76–81.5 [86.5–91.5, 96.5–101.5, 106.5–112]cm)

Finished size: 36 (38, 42, 46)" (91.5 [96.5, 106.5, 117]cm)

MATERIALS
8 balls Crystal Palace Chenille (1¾ oz [50g]/98 yds [90m]; 100% mercerized cotton), (4) medium#1058 Bleached White (MC)

For appliqués (optional): 1 ball each of #1219 Fushia (A), #2342 Lime (B), #4043 Green (C), #1317 Yellow (D), #9784 Red (E), #9660 Purple (F), and a trace amount of #9598 Black (G)

1 pair US 6 (4mm) needles or size required to achieve gauge

1 pair US 9 (5.5mm) needles or size required to achieve gauge

1 set of 4 US 6 (4mm) double-pointed needles

12" (30.5cm) white 2.5mm-thick cord

5 stitch holders

GAUGE
17 stitches and 26 rows = 4" (10cm) in seed stitch with smaller needles

8 stitches and 10 rows = 4" (10cm) in pattern with larger needles

STITCH PATTERN
MESH STITCH
Row 1 (RS): K1, *yo twice, k1; repeat from * to end.
Row 2: *K1, (k1, p1) into double yo, then pass the 2 knit stitches over the purl stitch; repeat from * to last st, k1.
Repeat rows 1–2 for Mesh Stitch.

Note The instructions are written for the smallest size. When changes are necessary for larger sizes, those instructions are enclosed in parentheses.

Back

With larger needles and MC, cast on 37 (39, 43, 47) stitches loosely.

Work in Mesh Stitch until the Back measures 19 (20, 21, 22)" (48 [51, 53.5, 56]cm) from the cast-on edge, ending with RS facing for next row.

Change to smaller needles and proceed as follows:

Next row (RS) K1, *yo, k1; repeat from * to end—73 (77, 85, 93) stitches.

Next Row Purl, decreasing 4 (4, 6, 6) stitches evenly across—69 (73, 79, 87) stitches.

Next Row K1, *p1, k1; repeat from * to end.

Repeat the last row once more for seed stitch.

ARMHOLE SHAPING

Continuing in seed stitch, bind off 4 stitches at the beginning of the next 2 rows—61 (65, 71, 79) stitches.

Continue even in seed stitch until the armhole measures 9½ (10, 10½, 11)" (24 [25.5, 26.5, 28]cm), ending with RS facing for next row.

SHOULDER SHAPING

Bind off 6 (6, 6, 7) stitches at the beginning of the next 4 rows, then 5 (6, 6, 7) stitches on the following 2 rows. Bind off the remaining 27 (29, 35, 37) stitches.

Left Front

***With larger needles and MC, cast on 19 (19, 21, 23) stitches loosely.

Work from ** to ** as given for the Back.

Change to smaller needles and proceed as follows:

Next row (RS) K1, *yo, k1; repeat from * to end—37 (37, 41, 45) stitches.

Next Row Purl, decreasing 2 (2, 4, 4) stitches evenly across—35 (35, 37, 41) stitches.***

Work 2 rows in seed stitch as given for the Back, ending with RS facing for next row.

ARMHOLE SHAPING

Next row (RS): Bind off 4 stitches, work in seed stitch to end of row—31 (31, 33, 37) stitches.

NECK SHAPING

Decrease 1 stitch at the neck edge on every 2nd row 14 (13, 15, 16) times—17 (18, 18, 21) stitches. Continue in seed stitch until the armhole measures 9½ (10, 10½, 11)" (24 [25.5, 26.5, 28]cm), ending with RS facing for next row.

SHOULDER SHAPING

Bind off 6 (6, 6, 7) stitches at the beginning of the next 2 alternate rows. Work 1 row even. Bind off remaining stitches.

Right Front

Work from *** to *** as given for the Left Front.

Work 3 rows in seed stitch as given for the Back, ending with WS facing for next row.

ARMHOLE SHAPING

Next Row (WS): Bind off 4 stitches, work in seed stitch to end—31 (31, 33, 37) stitches.

NECK SHAPING

Decrease 1 stitch at the neck edge on the next 3 rows, then every 2nd row 17 (17, 19, 20) times—11 (12, 12, 14) stitches. Continue in seed stitch until the armhole measures

9½ (10, 10½, 11)" (24 [25.5, 26.5, 28]cm), ending with WS facing for next row.

SHOULDER SHAPING

Bind off 6 (6, 6, 7) stitches at the beginning of the next 2 alternate rows. Work 1 row even. Bind off remaining stitches.

Sleeves (Make 2)

With larger needles and MC, cast on 39 (41, 43, 49) stitches.

Work in Mesh Stitch as given for the Back until the Sleeve measures 12 (12½, 13, 13½)" (30.5 [32, 33, 34.5]cm) from the cast-on edge, ending with RS facing for next row.

Next Row K1, *yo, k1; repeat from * to end—77 (81, 85, 97) stitches.

Bind off purlwise. Place markers 1" (2.5cm) down from the bind-off edge along the sides.

Finishing

Sew the shoulder seams. Sew in the Sleeves, placing Sleeves above markers along the 4 bind-off stitches of the Back and Front. Sew the side and Sleeve seams.

Sew the cord to the front opening. Make appliqués (page 49) and sew on as pictured.

Intro to Lace

Lace is a series of increases and decreases. The increases, yarn overs, form the holes of the lace. To compensate for the increases and keep the work even, you have to have the same number of decreases in a row. The easier laces usually have purling on the wrong side. You will eventually memorize the pattern as pianists do a tune; your fingers learn the rhythm. As you get comfortable with lace knitting, you can try more complicated lace stitches that have increasing and decreasing on both sides of the work!

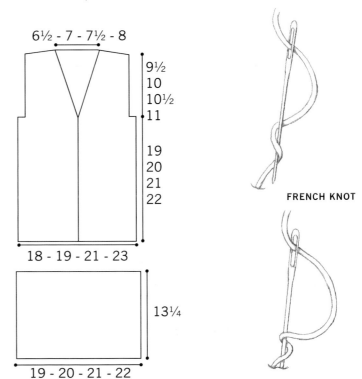

6½ - 7 - 7½ - 8

9½
10
10½
11

19
20
21
22

18 - 19 - 21 - 23

13¼

19 - 20 - 21 - 22

FRENCH KNOT

Appliqués

RED FLOWER WITH FUCHSIA CENTER (MAKE 2)

With E and smaller needles, cast on 3 stitches.

Row 1 (RS) Kf&b, knit to last st, kf&b—5 stitches.

Row 2 and All WS Rows Purl.

Row 3 As for row 1—7 stitches.

Row 5 As for row 1—9 stitches.

Row 7 Knit.

Row 9 Ssk, knit to last 2 stitches, k2tog—7 stitches. Place all stitches on a stitch holder.

Repeat 4 more times for 5 petals total.

Place the petals on 3 double-pointed needles as follows—needle 1: 12 stitches, needle 2: 11 stitches, needle 3: 12 stitches. With A, join the petals to work in the round.

Rnd 1 *Ssk, k3, k2tog; repeat from * to end of round—25 stitches.

Rnd 2 *Ssk, k1, k2tog; repeat from * to end of round—15 stitches.

Rnd 3 K1, *k2tog; repeat from * to end of round. 8 stitches. Cut long end and thread through remaining stitches. Secure.

With G, make 3 French knots at the center.

Repeat for purple (F) flower with fuchsia (A) center (make 2).

BLACK-EYED SUSAN (MAKE 4)

With D and smaller needles, cast on 1 stitch.

Row 1 (RS) Kf&b&f—3 stitches.

Rows 2 and 4 Purl.

Row 3 Kf&b, k1, kf&b—5 stitches.

Work 6 rows in stockinette stitch.

Row 11 Ssk, knit to last 2 stitches, k2tog—3 stitches. Place all stitches on a stitch holder.

Repeat 4 more times for 5 petals total.

Place petals on double-pointed needles with RS facing for next row—15 stitches.

Next Row With G, k1, *k2tog; repeat from * to end of row—8 stitches.

Applique

You can knit any kind of appliqué to sew onto your knitting, and these flowers can easily decorate a skirt or knapsack.

Next Row *P2tog; repeat from * to end of row—4 stitches.

Cut long end and thread through remaining stitches. Secure.

LEAF (MAKE 4 EACH IN B AND C)

With smaller needles, cast on 5 stitches.

Row 1 (RS) K2, yo, k1, yo, k2—7 stitches.

Row 2 and All WS Rows Purl.

Row 3 K3, yo, k1, yo, k3—9 stitches.

Row 5 K4, yo, k1, yo, k4—11 stitches.

Row 7 Ssk, k7, k2tog—9 stitches.

Row 9 Ssk, k5, k2tog—7 stitches.

Row 11 Ssk, k3, k2tog—5 stitches.

Row 13 Ssk, k1, k2tog—3 stitches.

Row 15 Sl1, k2tog, psso—1 stitch. Fasten off.

VINE (MAKE 2)

With C and double-pointed needles, cast on 4 stitches. Work I-cord (see page 17) for 7" (18cm), increasing 1 stitch on the last row. 5 stitches. Purl 1 row. Work Rows 1–15 of Leaf. Attach 4 of the leaves made previously to the vine along its length.

APRIL

DEADLINES FOR MAGAZINE or yarn company winter publications are usually due in May, which makes April my month for designing and swatching. The work has a quiet nature, which suits me, because I have a quiet nature, too. Magazines and yarn companies give me themes to create from. I read through the themes and make sketches of whatever ideas pop into my head. If the themes don't inspire me, picking up a colorful ball of sumptuous wool will! Those are the good days.

Like writer's block, however, there is such a thing as designer's block. When that happens, I do some more research of my own. I find magazines (fashion and home décor) somewhat helpful; I really enjoy interpreting graphic patterns into knitwear. The Internet also offers a plethora of color, pattern, fashion, and style. The trick is to always have the sketchbook handy to record any ideas that I get.

I try to submit approximately eight designs. If I am lucky, one may get selected; I am doubly fortunate if they select two. When the designs are returned to me after a few months, I can see clearly why some were rejected and some were kept for future consideration. (I will never forget the gray cabled sweater I did with red flames around the bottom—what was I thinking?) Sometimes a gem that I know in my heart to be a winner is rejected for whatever reason. Reworked with different yarn, one past rejection became my best-selling kit. I never weed my own submissions of designs I may only feel so-so about—I let the editors select what they need, and I give them an array of choices. It is those perfect fits that have me dancing around the house, squealing like an idiot, because something I have created has been recognized and liked. That, and the sense of satisfaction when a design appears nicely photo-graphed in a magazine, keep me going.

52

55

57

You can't wait for inspiration. You have to go after it with a club.
—JACK LONDON
(1876–1916)

Flower Power Felted Shopping Bag

This project introduces two new techniques: felting and intarsia. Intarsia is different from Fair Isle in that you work blocks of color rather than carrying yarn that is not being used across the row. With intarsia, you twist the new yarn around the old yarn before you bring it into action. This is a fun project with rewarding results.

Beginner

SIZE
13" x 15" (33cm x 38cm)

MATERIALS
Alafoss Lopi Lett (3½ oz [100g]/109 yds [99m]; 100% wool) [4] medium
  6 balls #9432 Grape Heather (MC)
  1 ball #1411 Sun Yellow (A)
  1 ball #1408 Light Red Heather (B)

1 pair US 8 (5mm) needles or size required to achieve gauge

1 pair of US 8 (5mm) double-pointed needles

Two ¾–1" (19–25mm) diameter wooden or bamboo dowels, 15" (38cm) long

5" x 15" (12.5cm x 38cm) piece of buckram stiffener for finished base

40" (1m) piece of fabric for lining

GAUGE
16 stitches and 20 rows = 4" (10cm) in stockinette stitch

needle, and then I knit the final stitch in the old color (bringing it over the new yarn). This prevents a hole from appearing. Then, I bring the working yarn to the left of the work (above the new color), and pull up the new color to begin working. For the following rows, I repeat this last step of bringing the new yarn from beneath, thereby twisting the yarns to prevent holes.

Front, Back, and Base (1 Piece)

With straight needles and MC, cast on 77 stitches. Beginning with a knit row, work 8 rows in stockinette stitch.

Next row (RS) Purl (turning ridge).

Beginning with a purl row, work in stockinette stitch until the work measures 28½" (72.5cm) from the turning ridge, ending with RS facing for next row.

Next Row K12, knit row 1 of Flower Chart across next 53 stitches (reading row from right to left), knit to end.

Note When changing colors, I introduce the new yarn 1 stitch before I want to use it. I "lock" it in by laying it over the left

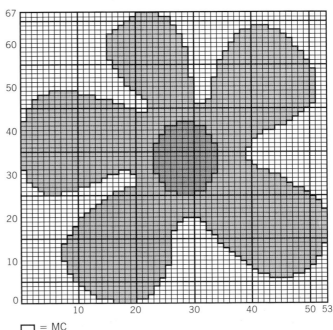

☐ = MC

▨ = A

▨ = B

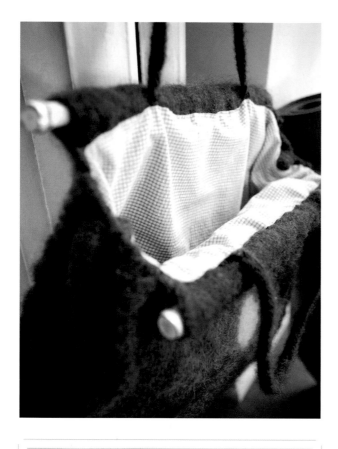

Next Row P12, purl row 2 of Flower Chart (reading row from left to right), purl to end of row.

Flower Chart is now set. Continue working Flower Chart to the end of the chart.

With MC, continue in stockinette stitch for 2¼" (5.5cm) from top of chart, ending with RS facing for next row.

Next Row Purl (turning ridge).

Beginning with a purl row, work 8 rows in stockinette stitch. Bind off all stitches.

Sides (Make 2)

With straight needles and MC, cast on 26 stitches.

Work in stockinette stitch until the Side measures 17¾" (45cm) from the cast-on edge. Bind off all stitches.

Handles (Make 2)

With double-pointed needles and MC, cast on 5 stitches. *Do not turn. With RS facing, slide these 5 stitches to the other end of the needle. Pull tight and knit these 5 stitches. Repeat from * until I-cord handle measures 20¾" (52.5cm). Bind off all stitches.

Finishing

Felt pieces by placing them in a mesh laundry bag with an old towel (or washcloth) and dropping them into the washing machine. Add 1 tablespoon (15ml) of detergent and 1 teaspoon (5ml) of baking soda. Set the machine for the smallest load and the hottest cycle. A hot wash with cold rinse cycle should produce the desired results, but check periodically for shrinkage.

Block the pieces to the following measurements:

Front, Back, and Base: 31" x 15" x 5" (78.5cm x 38cm x 12.5cm)

Sides: 5" x 13" (12.5cm x 33cm)

Handles: 1¾" x 16" (4.5cm x 40.5cm)

Sew the Sides to the Front, Base, and Back using blanket stitch (see illustration). Sew the Handles to the top of the bag. Fold the Sides at the top to form three pleats, and sew through all layers to secure. Cut buckram stiffener to size, and sew to base. Sew in the lining.

Felting

Different yarns will give different results when felted. Not all wool felts equally. The yarns I have used for felting projects in this book (the Flower Power Felted Shopping Bag, shown here, and Turtle Doves, page 139) both felt very well but differently. Blocking is the key to shaping your item evenly. You can stretch the fabric to size while it's still damp. Pin it to the measurements and let it air-dry.

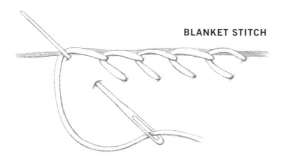

BLANKET STITCH

Bookworm Bookmark

There is nothing more pleasing to knit than a small project with a big result. This ethereal bookmark has an old-world antique feeling. Give this bookmark with a gift of books to make your gift that much more personal.

Intermediate

SIZE
8½" x 2" (22cm x 5cm)

MATERIALS
1 ball Needful Yarns Lana Gatto Mohair Royal (1 oz [25g]/235 yds [215m];80% kid mohair/20% nylon) #12921 Pink, **(1)** super fine

1 pair US 0 (2mm) needles or size required to achieve gauge

GAUGE
41 stitches and 47 rows = 4" (10cm) in stockinette stitch

STITCH PATTERN
TULIP LACE STITCH

Row 1 (RS): Sl1, k2tog, yo, k5, yo, sl1, k2tog, psso, yo, k5, yo, sl1, k1, psso, k1.
Row 2 and All WS Rows: Purl.
Row 3: As for row 1.
Row 5: Sl1, k2, *yo, sl1, k1, psso, k1, k2tog, yo, k3; repeat from * to end of row.
Row 7: Sl2, k1, p2sso, yo, k1, yo, sl1, k2tog, psso, yo, k1, yo, sl1, k2tog, psso, yo, k1, yo, sl1, k2tog, psso, yo, k1, yo, sl1, k1, psso, k1.
Row 8: Purl.

Bookmark

Cast on 19 stitches.

Knit 4 rows.

Work Tulip Lace Stitch until the work measures 8" (20.5cm) from the cast-on edge, ending with RS facing for next row.

Next Row Ssk, k17, k2tog.

Next Row Ssk, k15, k2tog.

Continue to decrease 1 stitch at each end of the needle every row until there are 3 stitches remaining.

Next Row K3tog. Fasten off.

TASSEL (MAKE 1)
Wind yarn 16 times around your hand. Break the yarn, leaving a long tail, and thread through a tapestry needle. Slip the needle through the loops and tie tightly. Wind yarn 1" (2.5cm) below the fold. Secure. Cut through the loops and trim evenly. Attach the tassel to the end of the bookmark.

Working with Mohair
Fine mohair yarn is best worked loosely to allow the hairs to fill into the work, giving it a cobwebby look.

Stitch Therapy Turtleneck

You may have heard of knitting as the new yoga, but have you heard of it as the new therapy? I'm kidding, but I do tend to lose myself when using many stitches in design. There is nothing like knitting to make you forget about whatever it is you need to do, at least for a little while. Consider it a retreat from work, commitments, or housework. Soon you will be lost in the rhythm of stitches.

Experienced

SIZE
Small (Medium, Large, X-Large)

Bust: 30–32 (34–36, 38–40, 42–44)" (76–81.5 [86.5–91.5, 96.5–101.5, 106.5–112]cm)

Finished size: 35 (38, 43, 47)" (89 [96.5, 109, 119.5]cm)

MATERIALS
13 (13, 14, 15) hanks Classic Elite Yarns Renaissance (1¾ oz [50g]/110 yds [100m]; 100% wool) #7173 Tuscan Field, (3) light

1 pair US 6 (4mm) needles

1 pair US 7 (4.5mm) needles or size required to achieve gauge

1 cable needle

2 stitch holders

GAUGE
20 stitches and 26 rows = 4" (10cm) in stockinette stitch with larger needles

STITCH PATTERNS
DOUBLE WAVE CABLE PATTERN

Row 1 (RS): K2, (p2, k2) 3 times.
Row 2: P2, (k2, p2) 3 times.
Row 3: T6B, p2, t6b.
Row 4: As for row 2.
Row 5: As for row 1.
Rows 6–9: Repeat rows 4–5 twice.
Row 10: As for row 2.
Row 11: K2, p2, t6f, p2, k2.
Row 12: As for row 2.
Row 13: As for row 1.

Rows 14–15: Repeat rows 12–13 once.
Row 16: As for row 2.
Repeat rows 1–16 for Double Wave Cable Pattern.

LOBSTER CLAW PATTERN

Row 1 (RS): K2, p4, k2.
Row 2: P2, k4, p2.
Row 3: C4F, c4b.
Row 4: Purl.
Rows 5–8: Repeat rows 1–2 twice.
Repeat rows 1–8 for Lobster Claw Pattern.

Note The instructions are written for the smallest size. When changes are necessary for larger sizes, those instructions are enclosed in parentheses.

Back

**With smaller needles, cast on 94 (106, 118, 126) stitches.

Row 1 (RS) K2, *p2, k2; repeat from * to end of row.

Row 2 P2, *k2, p2; repeat from * to end of row.

Repeat rows 1–2 for ribbing until the Back measures 3" (7.5cm) from the cast-on edge, ending with RS facing for next row and increasing 10 (8, 10, 16) stitches evenly across the last row—104 (114, 128, 142) stitches.

Change to larger needles and proceed as follows:

Row 1 K2 (2, 0, 2), (p3, k2) 1 (2, 0, 1) time(s), p3, [work row 1 of Lobster Claw Pattern, p3, k2, p3, work row 1 of Double Wave Cable Pattern, p3, k2, p3] 2 (2, 3, 3) times, work row 1 of Lobster Claw Pattern, p3, (k2, p3) 1 (2, 0, 1) time(s), k2 (2, 0, 2).

Row 2 K10 (15, 3, 10), [work row 2 of Lobster Claw Pattern, k8, work row 2 of Double Wave Cable Pattern, k8] 2 (2, 3, 3) times, work row 2 of Lobster Claw Pattern, knit to end.

Row 3 K2 (2, 0, 2), (p3, k2) 1 (2, 0, 1) time(s), p3, [work row 3 of Lobster Claw Pattern, p3, k2, p3, work row 3 of Double Wave Cable Pattern, p3, k2, p3] 2 (2, 3, 3) times, work row 3 of Lobster Claw Pattern, p3, (k2, p3) 1 (2, 0, 1) time(s), k2 (2, 0, 2).

Row 4 K10 (15, 3, 10), [work row 4 of Lobster Claw Pattern, k8, work row 2 of Double Wave Cable Pattern, k8] 2 (2, 3, 3) times, work row 4 of Lobster Claw Pattern, knit to end.

Pattern is now set. Continue in pattern until the Back measures 14½ (15, 16, 16½)" (37 [38, 40.5, 42]cm) from the cast-on edge, ending with RS facing for next row.

ARMHOLE SHAPING

Next Row Bind off 8 (8, 11, 8) stitches at the beginning of the next 2 rows—88 (98, 106, 126) stitches.**

Tracking Stitches

To help remember where stitch patterns begin and end, place markers at the beginning and end of a repeat. Markers can be store-bought rings, but I prefer to make my own using scrap yarn in a different color tied into a small loop, as these homemade markers tend not to slip off the needles.

Continue in pattern until the armhole measures 9½ (10, 10½, 11)" (24 [25.5, 26.5, 28]cm), ending with RS facing for next row.

SHOULDER SHAPING

Bind off 9 (10, 11, 14) stitches at the beginning of the next 4 rows, then bind off 8 (10, 10, 13) stitches at the beginning of the following 2 rows. Leave the remaining 36 (38, 42, 44) stitches on a stitch holder for the Back neck.

Front

Work from ** to ** as given for the Back.

Continue in pattern until the armhole measures 6½ (7, 7½, 8)" (16.5 [18, 19, 20.5]cm), ending with RS facing for next row.

NECK SHAPING (LEFT SIDE)

Pattern across first 38 (43, 46, 56) stitches. Place remaining stitches on a spare needle. Turn. Continuing in pattern, decrease 1 stitch at the neck edge every row 12 (13, 14, 15) times, ending with RS facing for next row—26 (30, 32, 41) stitches.

Continue in pattern until the armhole measures 9½ (10, 10½, 11)" (24 [25.5, 26.5, 28]cm), ending with RS facing for next row.

SHOULDER SHAPING (LEFT SIDE)

Bind off 9 (10, 11, 14) stitches at the beginning of the next 2 alternate rows. Work 1 row even in pattern. Bind off the remaining stitches.

NECK SHAPING (RIGHT SIDE)

With RS facing, slip the next 12 (12, 14, 14) stitches from the spare needle onto a stitch holder. Work in pattern on the remaining stitches to the end. Continue to decrease 1 stitch at the neck edge every row 12 (13, 14, 15) times—26 (30, 32, 41) stitches.

Continue in pattern until the armhole measures 9 (9½, 10, 10½)" (23 [24, 25.5, 26.5]cm), ending with WS facing for next row.

SHOULDER SHAPING (RIGHT SIDE)

Bind off 9 (10, 11, 14) stitches at the beginning of the next 2 alternate rows. Work 1 row even in pattern. Bind off remaining stitches.

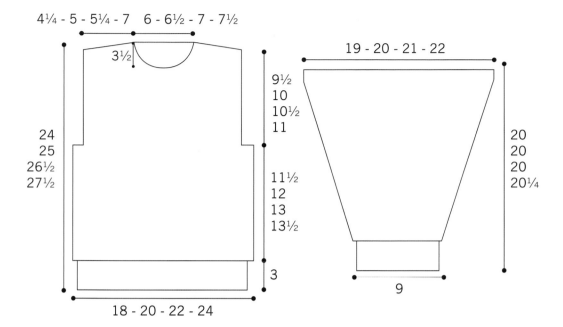

Sleeves (Make 2)

With smaller needles, cast on 54 stitches.

Work in (k2, p2) ribbing as given for the Back for 3" (7.5cm), ending with RS facing for next row.

Change to larger needles and proceed as follows:

Row 1 (RS) K1, p3, work row 1 of Lobster Claw Pattern, p3, k2, p3, work row 1 of Double Wave Cable Pattern, p3, k2, p3, work row 1 of Lobster Claw Pattern, p3, k1.

Row 2 K4, work row 2 of Lobster Claw Pattern, k8, work row 2 of Double Wave Cable Pattern, k8, work row 2 of Lobster Claw Pattern, k4.

Row 3 K1, M1L, p3, work row 3 of Lobster Claw Pattern, p3, k2, p3, work row 3 of Double Wave Cable Pattern, p3, k2, p3, work row 3 of Lobster Claw Pattern, p3, M1R, k1—56 stitches.

Row 4 K5, work row 4 of Lobster Claw Pattern, k8, work row 2 of Double Wave Cable Pattern, k8, work row 4 of Lobster Claw Pattern, k5.

Row 5 K1, M1L, k1, p3, work row 5 of Lobster Claw Pattern, p3, k2, p3, work row 5 of Double Wave Cable Pattern, p3, k2, p3, work row 5 of Lobster Claw Pattern, p3, k1, M1R, k1—58 stitches.

Row 6 K6, work row 6 of Lobster Claw Pattern, k8, work row

6 of Double Wave Cable Pattern, k8, work row 4 of Lobster Claw Pattern, k6. Patterns are now in position.

Continue in pattern, AT THE SAME TIME continue to increase 1 stitch at each end of the needle on every alternate row to 94 (106, 118, 130) stitches, then every 4th row to 114 (120, 126, 132) stitches, taking increased stitches into the pattern. Continue even until the Sleeve measures 20 (20, 20, 20¼)" (51 [51, 51, 51.5]cm) from the cast-on edge. Bind off all stitches.

Finishing

Block the pieces to the measurements.

Sew the left shoulder seam.

NECKBAND

With smaller needles and RS facing, pick up and knit 17 (18, 17, 18) stitches down the left front neck. Knit across 12 (12, 14, 14) stitches from the stitch holder. Pick up and knit 17 (18, 17, 18) stitches up the right Front neck. Knit across 36 (38, 42, 44) stitches from the Back neck stitch holder—82 (86, 90, 94) stitches. Work in (k2, p2) ribbing as given for the Back for 8" (20cm). Bind off in ribbing.

Sew the right shoulder seam. Sew in the Sleeves. Sew the sleeve and side seams. Fold the neckband to the inside and whipstitch (see page 65) into place.

MAY

AS A WAY TO PRACTICE writing and as a record of my experience writing this book, I started a blog. It soon developed into a to-do list and an account of what was going on in my life. There is a fabulous exchange of ideas, methods, and information in the "blogosphere"—especially for knitters. I am amazed at the sheer talent and ingenuity of so many of those knitters out there. Blogging is a wonderful way to keep in touch and communicate with the knitting community.

Anything you want to know about knitting (or almost anything else) is at your fingertips. It is a virtual key to knowledge. I like to see what fashions are new on the runways, styles of photography, or how a blogger might interpret a design. The interesting thing about blogging is that there is a fantastic exchange between people, not only on your own continent, but worldwide. An opinion is stated, another one given—an idea is born and then interpreted. Friendships develop.

To acquire knowledge, one must study; but to acquire wisdom, one must observe.
—MARILYN VOS SAVANT (1946–)

62

67

71

Little Boy Blue Cardigan

Designing for little ones is fun. You can make the patterns colorful, intricate, or simple and the kids always look adorable. I am a great fan of classic designs, and this one is timeless.

Beginner

SIZE

Age: 2 (4, 6, 8, 10) years

Chest: 21 (23, 25, 26½, 28)" (53.5 [58.5, 63.5, 67.5, 71]cm)

Finished chest: 26 (28, 30, 32, 34)" (66 [71, 76, 81.5, 86.5]cm)

MATERIALS

4 (5, 6, 7, 8) balls Rowan All Seasons Cotton (1¾ oz [50 g]/100 yds [90m]; 60% cotton/40% acrylic) #199 Ravish, (4) medium

1 pair US 6 (4mm) needles

1 pair US 7 (4.5mm) needles or size needed to obtain gauge

1 stitch holder

Five ⅔" (15mm) buttons

GAUGE

16 stitches and 24 rows = 4" (10cm) in stockinette stitch with larger needles

Note The instructions are written for the smallest size. When changes are necessary for larger sizes, those instructions are enclosed in parentheses.

Back

With smaller needles, cast on 46 (50, 54, 58, 62) stitches.

Row 1 (RS) K2, *p2, k2; repeat from * to end of row.

Row 2 P2, *k2, p2; repeat from * to end of row.

Repeat rows 1–2 for ribbing for 2 (2½, 2½, 3, 3)" (5 [6, 6, 7.5, 7.5]cm), ending with RS facing for next row and increasing 6 stitches evenly across the last row—52 (56, 60, 64, 68) stitches.

Change to larger needles and work in stockinette stitch until the Back measures 5¾ (6, 6½, 8, 9½)" (14.5 [15, 16.5, 20.5, 24]cm) from the cast-on edge, ending with RS facing for next row.

ARMHOLE SHAPING

Bind off 4 (5, 5, 5, 6) stitches at the beginning of the next 2 rows—44 (46, 50, 54, 56) stitches.

Continue even until the Back measures 11¾ (12½, 13½, 15½, 17)" (30 [32, 34.5, 39.5, 43]cm) from the cast-on edge, ending with RS facing for next row.

SHOULDER SHAPING

Bind off 4 (5, 5, 6, 7) stitches at the beginning of the next 2 rows, then 5 (5, 6, 7, 7) stitches at the beginning of the next 2 rows. Place the remaining 26 (26, 28, 28, 28) stitches on a stitch holder.

Left Front

**With smaller needles, cast on 22 (26, 26, 30, 30) stitches.

Work in (k2, p2) ribbing as given for the Back for 2 (2½, 2½, 3, 3)" (5 [6, 6, 7.5, 7.5]cm), ending with RS facing for next row and increasing 4 (2, 4, 2, 4) stitches evenly across the last row—26 (28, 30, 32, 34) stitches.**

Change to larger needles and work in stockinette stitch until the Left Front measures 5¾ (6, 6½, 8, 9½)" (14.5 [15, 16.5, 20.5, 24]cm) from the cast-on edge, ending with RS facing for next row.

ARMHOLE SHAPING

Next Row Bind off 4 (5, 5, 5, 6) stitches, knit to end of row—22 (23, 25, 27, 28) stitches.

Continue even until the Left Front measures 9¼ (10, 10½, 12½, 14)" (23.5 [25.5, 26.5, 32, 35.5]cm) from the cast-on edge, ending with WS facing for next row.

NECK SHAPING

Next Row Bind off 4 (4, 4, 5, 5) stitches, purl to end of row—18 (19, 21, 22, 23) stitches.

Decrease 1 stitch at the neck edge on the next and every row until there are 9 (10, 11, 13, 14) stitches remaining.

Continue even in stockinette stitch until the Left Front measures 11¾ (12½, 13½, 15½, 17)" (30 [32, 34.5, 39.5, 43]cm) from the cast-on edge, ending with RS facing for next row.

SHOULDER SHAPING

Bind off 4 (5, 5, 6, 7) stitches at the beginning of the next row. Work 1 row even. Bind off remaining 5 (5, 6, 7, 7) stitches.

Right Front

Work from ** to ** as given for the Left Front.

Change to larger needles and work in stockinette stitch until the Right Front measures 6¾ (6, 6½, 8, 9½)" (17 [15, 16.5, 20.5, 24]cm) from the cast-on edge, ending with WS facing for next row.

ARMHOLE SHAPING

Continue even until the Right Front measures 9¼ (10, 10½, 12½, 14)" (23.5 [25.5, 26.5, 32, 35.5]cm) from the cast-on edge, ending with RS facing for next row.

NECK SHAPING

Next Row Bind off 4 (4, 4, 5, 5) stitches, knit to end of row—18 (19, 21, 22, 23) stitches.

Decrease 1 stitch at the neck edge on the next and every row until there are 9 (10, 11, 13, 14) stitches remaining.

Continue even in stockinette stitch until the Right Front measures 11¾ (12½, 13½, 15½, 17)" (30 [32, 34.5, 39.5, 43]cm) from the cast-on edge, ending with WS facing for next row.

SHOULDER SHAPING

Next Row Bind off 4 (5, 5, 6, 7) stitches, purl to end of row. Work 1 row even. Bind off remaining 5 (5, 6, 7, 7) stitches.

Sleeves (Make 2)

With smaller needles, cast on 30 (30, 30, 34, 34) stitches.

Work in (k2, p2) ribbing as given for the Back for 2 (2½, 2½, 3, 3)" (5 [6, 6, 7.5, 7.5]cm), ending with RS facing for next row and increasing 2 (4, 4, 2, 2) stitches evenly across the last row—32 (34, 34, 36, 36) stitches.

Change to larger needles and work in stockinette stitch, increasing 1 stitch at each end of the needle on the 3rd and following 4th rows to 36 (42, 48, 54, 54) stitches then every 6th row to 48 (52, 56, 60, 60) stitches.

Continue in stockinette stitch until the Sleeve measures 8 (11, 12, 13, 14½)" (20.5 [28, 30.5, 33, 37]cm) from the cast-on edge, ending with RS facing for next row. Bind off.

Pocket

With larger needles, cast on 14 stitches.

Work in stockinette stitch for 2½ (3, 3, 3¼, 3¼)" (6 [7.5, 7.5, 8.5, 8.5]cm), ending with RS facing for next row. Change to smaller needles and work in (k2, p2) ribbing as given for the Back for 4 rows. Bind off in ribbing.

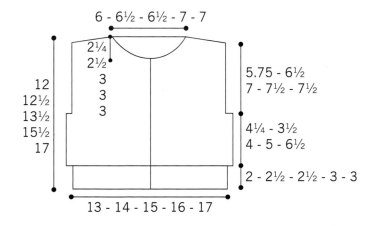

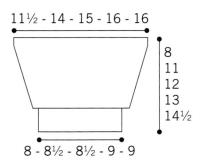

Finishing

Pin all pieces to measurements and cover with a damp cloth. Leave the cloth to dry on garment.

Sew the shoulder seams. Sew the pocket into place using whipstitch (see below).

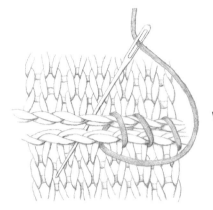

WHIPSTITCH

BUTTONHOLE BAND

With RS facing and smaller needles, pick up and knit 38 (38, 42, 50, 54) stitches down the Left Front edge.

Work in (k2, p2) ribbing as given for the Back for 3 rows.

Row 4 (RS): Work 2 stitches in rib, *yo, k2tog (buttonhole made), rib 6 (6, 7, 8, 10) stitches; repeat from * 3 times, bind off 2 stitches, rib to end.

Work 3 rows in ribbing. Bind off.

BUTTON BAND

With RS facing and smaller needles, pick up and knit 38 (38, 42, 50, 54) stitches down the Right Front edge.

Work in (k2, p2) ribbing as given for the Back for 7 rows. Bind off.

Sew in the sleeves. Sew the side and Sleeve seams. Sew on the buttons, matching them to the buttonholes.

COLLAR

With RS of work facing and smaller needles, starting at the center of the buttonband, pick up and knit 16 (18, 21, 23, 23) stitches up the Right Front neck edge. Knit 26 (26, 28, 28, 28) stitches from the Back neck stitch holder. Pick up and knit 16 (18, 21, 23, 23) stitches down the Left Front neck edge, ending at the center point of buttonhole band—58 (62, 70, 74, 74) stitches.

Work in (k2, p2) ribbing as given for the Back for 4" (10cm). Bind off in ribbing.

Kids' Knits

When knitting for kids, consider the yarn carefully. It has to be comfortable for them to wear and have enough "give" that it moves with them when they move. Fibers blended with acrylic wash well, always a plus for kids' wear! Rowan has always made fantastic yarn in superb color choices—the All Seasons Cotton is enough to keep the wearer warm without overheating active tykes.

Auction Morning Cardie

Scoring a big bargain is a great way to start a Saturday morning. The Auction Cardie will keep the chill off from the morning air.

Intermediate

SIZE
Small (Medium, Large, X-Large)

Bust: 30–32 (34–36, 38–40, 42–44)" (76–81 [86–91, 97–102, 107–112]cm)

Finished size: 35 (39, 43, 47)" (89 [99, 109, 125.75]cm)

MATERIALS
12 (13, 14, 15) balls Mission Falls 1824 Cotton (1¾ oz [50g]/ 84 yds [77m]; 100% cotton) #7616 Sage, (**4**) medium

1 pair US 6 (4mm) needles

1 pair US 7 (4.5mm) needles or size required to obtain gauge

1 36" (90cm) US 6 (4mm) circular needle

1 stitch holder

Five ⅔" (15mm) buttons

GAUGE
18 stitches and 24 rows = 4" (10cm) in stockinette stitch with larger needles

---

Note The instructions are written for the smallest size. When changes are necessary for larger sizes, those instructions are enclosed in parentheses.

Back

With smaller needles, cast on 74 (84, 92, 102) stitches.

Row 1 (RS) *K1, p1; repeat from * to end of row.

Repeat row 1 for seed stitch for 1½" (4cm), increasing 4 stitches evenly across the last row and ending with RS facing for next row—78 (88, 96, 106) stitches.

Change to larger needles and work in stockinette stitch until the Back measures 12½ (13, 13½, 14)" (32 [33, 34.5, 35.5]cm) from the cast-on edge, ending with RS facing for next row.

ARMHOLE SHAPING
Bind off 5 stitches at the beginning of the next 2 rows—68 (78, 86, 96) stitches.

Continue even until the armhole measures 8 (8½, 9, 9½)" (20.5 [21.5, 23, 24]cm), ending with RS facing for next row.

SHOULDER SHAPING
Bind off 6 (7, 9, 10) stitches at the beginning of the next 4 rows, then 6 (8, 8, 10) stitches at the beginning of the following 2 rows. Leave the remaining 32 (34, 34, 36) stitches on a stitch holder.

Left Front

**With smaller needles, cast on 38 (42, 46, 52) stitches.

Work in seed stitch as given for the Back for 1½" (4cm), increasing 2 stitches evenly across the last row, ending with RS facing for next row—40 (44, 48, 54) stitches.

Change to larger needles, and work in stockinette stitch for 6 rows.**

***Row 1 (RS)** K6 (10, 14, 20), *k3, k2tog, yo, k1, yo, ssk, k3,* k6; repeat from * to * once, k6.

Rows 2, 4, 6, 8 Purl.

Row 3 K6 (10, 14, 20), *k2, k2tog, yo, k3, yo, ssk, k2, k6; repeat from * to end of row.

Row 5 K6 (10, 14, 20), *k1, k2tog, yo, k5, yo, ssk, k1, k6; repeat from * to end of row.

Row 7 Knit.

Row 9 K6 (10, 14, 20), *k6, insert right-hand needle into first yo-space of 5th row and knit it, leaving long loop on the needle; repeat for first space of 3rd row and the next 4 yo-spaces, k5, k6; repeat from * to end of row.

Row 10 *P6, p5, p6tog, p6; repeat from * to end of row.

Row 11 Knit.

Row 12 Purl.***

Work 12 (14, 16, 18) rows in stockinette stitch and then proceed as follows:

Row 1 (RS) K14 (18, 22, 28) stitches, k3, k2tog, yo, k1, yo, ssk, k3, knit to end.

Rows 2, 4, 6, 8 Purl.

Row 3 K14 (18, 22, 28), k2, k2tog, yo, k3, yo, ssk, k2, knit to end.

Row 5 K14 (18, 22, 28), k1, k2tog, yo, k5, yo, ssk, k1, knit to end.

Row 7 Knit.

Row 9 K14 (18, 22, 28), k6, *insert right-hand needle into first space of 5th row and knit it, leaving long loop on needle; repeat from * for first space of 3rd row and the next 4 yo-spaces, knit to end.

Row 10 P20, p6tog, purl to end of row.

Row 11 Knit.

Row 12 Purl.

Work 12 (14, 16, 18) rows stockinette stitch.

Repeat from *** to *** once.

Continue in stockinette stitch until the Left Front measures 12½ (13, 13½, 14)" (32 [33, 34.5, 35.5]cm) from the cast-on edge, ending with RS facing for next row.

NECKLINE AND ARMHOLE SHAPING

Next Row Bind off 5 stitches, knit to end of row—35 (39, 43, 49) stitches.

Work 1 row even.

Decrease 1 stitch at the neck edge on the next and every following alternate row to 23 (29, 34, 38) stitches, then every 4th row to 18 (22, 26, 30) stitches.

Continue in stockinette stitch until the armhole measures 8 (8½, 9, 9½)" (20.5 [21.5, 23, 24]cm), ending with RS facing for next row.

SHOULDER SHAPING

Bind off 6 (7, 9, 10) stitches at the beginning of next and following alternate row. Work 1 row even. Bind off remaining 6 (8, 8, 10) stitches.

Right Front

Work from ** to ** as given for Left Front.

****Row 1 (RS)** K6, *k3, k2tog, yo, k1, yo, ssk, k3,* k6; repeat from * to * once, k6 (10, 14, 20).

Rows 2, 4, 6, 8 Purl.

Row 3 K6, *k2, k2tog, yo, k3, yo, ssk, k2,* k6; repeat from * to * once, k6 (10, 14, 20).

Row 5 K6, *k1, k2tog, yo, k5, yo, ssk, k1,* k6; repeat from * to * once, k6 (10, 14, 20).

Row 7 Knit.

Row 9 K6, *k6, insert right-hand needle into first yo-space of 5th row and knit it, leaving long loop on needle; repeat for

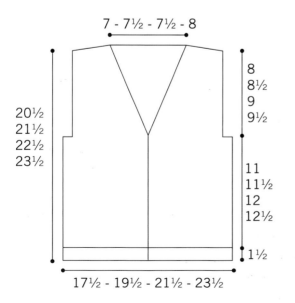

7 - 7½ - 7½ - 8

8
8½
9
9½

20½
21½
22½
23½

11
11½
12
12½

1½

17½ - 19½ - 21½ - 23½

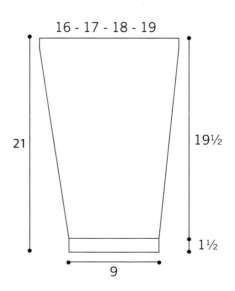

16 - 17 - 18 - 19

21

19½

1½

9

Row 9 K17, *k6, insert right-hand needle into first yo-space of 5th row and knit it, leaving long loop on needle; repeat for first space of 3rd row and the next 4 spaces, knit to end.

Row 10 P23 (27, 31, 37), p6tog, purl to end.

Row 11 Knit.

Row 12 Purl.

Work 12 (14, 16, 18) rows in stockinette stitch.

Repeat from **** to **** once.

Continue in stockinette stitch until the Right Front measures 12½ (13, 13½, 14)" (32 [33, 34.5, 35.5]cm) from the cast-on edge, ending with WS facing for next row.

NECKLINE AND ARMHOLE SHAPING

Next Row Bind off 5 stitches, purl to end of row—35 (39, 43, 49) stitches.

Decrease 1 stitch at the neck edge on next and every following alternate row to 23 (29, 34, 38) stitches, then every 4th row to 18 (22, 26, 30) stitches.

Continue in stockinette stitch until the armhole measures 8 (8½, 9, 9½)" (20.5 [21.5, 23, 24]cm), ending with WS facing for next row.

SHOULDER SHAPING

Bind off 6 (7, 9, 10) stitches at the beginning of the next 2 alternate rows. Work 1 row even. Bind off the remaining 6 (8, 8, 10) stitches.

1st space of 3rd row and the next 4 yo-spaces, k5,* k6; repeat from * to * once, k6 (10, 14, 20).

Row 10 P6 (10, 14, 20), *p5, p6tog, p6,* p6; repeat from * to * once, purl to end.

Row 11 Knit.

Row 12 Purl.****

Work 12 (14, 16, 18) rows in stockinette stitch and then proceed as follows:

Row 1 (RS) K12, k3, k2tog, yo, k1, yo, ssk, k3, knit to end.

Rows 2, 4, 6, 8 Purl.

Row 3 K17, k2, k2tog, yo, k3, yo, ssk, k2, knit to end.

Row 5 K17, k1, k2tog, yo, k5, yo, ssk, k1, knit to end.

Row 7 Knit.

Sleeves (Make 2)

With smaller needles, cast on 36 stitches.

Work in seed stitch as given for the Back for 1½" (4cm), increasing 2 stitches evenly across the last row and ending with RS facing for next row—38 stitches.

Change to larger needles and work in stockinette stitch, increasing 1 stitch at each end of the needle on the 3rd and following 6th (6th, 4th, 4th) rows to 64 (76, 52, 66) stitches.

Sizes S, L, and X-L only Increase 1 stitch at each end of the needle on every 8th (6th, 6th) row to 72 (80, 86) stitches.

All sizes Continue even in stockinette stitch until the Sleeve measures 21" (53.5cm) from the cast-on edge. Bind off all stitches.

Finishing

Pin all pieces to measurements and cover with a damp cloth.
Leave the cloth to dry on the garment.

FRONT AND NECK EDGING

Sew the shoulder seams. With RS of work facing and circular
needle, pick up and knit 73 (77, 81, 85) stitches up Right
Front edge, pick up and knit 36 (38, 40, 48) stitches up
Right Front neck edge. Knit 32 (34, 34, 36) stitches from the
back neck stitch holder. Pick up and knit 36 (38, 40, 48)
stitches down the Left Front neck edge. Pick up and knit 75
(78, 81, 84) stitches down the Left Front edge—250 (264,
276, 302) stitches.

Next Row (WS) Knit.

Next Row (Buttonhole Row) K2, *yo, k2tog, k15 (16, 17,
18); repeat from * 3 times, yo, k2tog, knit to end—5 buttonholes made.

Next 3 rows Knit.

Next row (RS) Bind off 73 (77, 81, 85) stitches to beginning
of neck shaping. *Sl remaining stitch onto left needle and
cast on 3 stitches using the cable cast-on method (page TK).
Bind off 7 stitches. Repeat from * to beginning of Left Front
neck shaping. Bind off remaining stitches.

Sew in the Sleeves. Sew the side and sleeve seams. Sew on
the buttons, matching them to the buttonholes.

Buttonholes

There are a couple of good ways to do
buttonholes. The Auction Morning Cardie
uses one method, which produces a small
buttonhole. If you would like to use larger
buttons, I recommend a different method.
Instead of working "yo, k2tog," bind off 2
stitches on this row, and when you come to
this location on the next row, cast on 2
stitches over the bound-off stitches.

The cable cast-on is a handy method
for casting on mid-project. Place the needle
and stitches you have just worked into your
left hand, thus turning the work. Slide
the right-hand needle between the first
and second stitches on the left-hand
needle, under the needle. Wrap the yarn
around as though to knit, and pull
through. Place this new stitch on the left-
hand needle. Repeat with the new stitch
acting as the first stitch and the next
stitch as the second, until you have cast on
the desired number of stitches.

Extraordinary Orchids Mother's Day Cardigan

This the meatiest project of the book, though it might not look it. To make this cardigan,
you have to like intarsia, and you have to like weaving in ends. For your efforts, you are rewarded
with what I think is the prettiest project in the book.

Experienced

SIZE
Small (Medium, Large, X-Large)

Bust: 30–32 (34–36, 38–40, 42–44) [76–81 [86–91, 97–102, 107–112]cm)

Finished size: 36 (40, 43, 49½)" (91.5 [101.5, 109, 125.75]cm)

MATERIALS
Classic Elite Yarns Four Seasons (1¾ [50g]/87 yds [80cm]; 70% cotton/30% wool)
(4) medium
13 (14, 15, 16) hanks

#7616 Natural (MC)
1 hank #7693 Everblue (A)
1 hank #7602 Yellow Daisy (B)
1 hank #7653 Very Berry (C),

1 pair US 8 (5mm) needles or size required to achieve gauge

1 36" (90cm) US 7 (4.5mm) circular needle

1 stitch holder

Five ¾" (18mm) buttons

GAUGE
20 stitches and 26 rows = 4" (10cm) in stockinette stitch with larger needles

STITCH PATTERNS
EDGING PATTERN

Row 1 (RS): *Ssk, k3tbl, yo, k1, yo, k3tbl, k2tog; repeat from * to end of row.
Row 2 and All WS Rows: Purl.
Row 3: *Ssk, k2tbl, yo, k1, yo, ssk, yo, k2tbl, k2tog; repeat from * to end of row.
Row 5: *Ssk, k1tbl, yo, k1, (yo, ssk) twice, yo, k1tbl, k2tog; repeat from * to end of row.
Row 7: *Ssk, yo, k1, (yo, ssk) 3 times, yo, k2tog; repeat from * to end of row.
Repeat rows 1–7 for the Edging.

PANEL PATTERN

Row 1 (RS): K2, p2, yon, sl1, k1, psso, k1, k2tog, yfrn, p2, k2.
Rows 2: K4, p5, k4.
Rows 3–6: Repeat rows 1–2 twice.
Row 7: K2, p2, k5, p2, k2.
Row 8: As for row 2.
Row 9: K2, p2, k2tog, yf, k1, yf, sl1, k1, psso, p2, k2.
Row 10: As for row 2.
Rows 11–14: Repeat rows 9–10 twice.
Row 15: As for row 7.
Row 16: As for row 2.
Repeat rows 1–16 for Panel Pattern.

Note The instructions are written for the smallest size. When changes are necessary for larger sizes, those instructions are enclosed in parentheses.

Back

With larger needles and MC, cast on 88 (99, 110, 121) stitches.

Work Edging Pattern once.

Knit 4 rows, increasing 5 (increasing 0, decreasing 3, increasing 2) stitches evenly across the last row—93 (99, 107, 123) stitches.

Proceed as follows:

Row 1 K1 (1, 2, 1), [work row 1 of Panel Pattern, k0 (1, 2, 5), work row 1 of Orchid Chart, k0 (1, 2, 5)] 3 times, work row 1 of Panel Pattern, k1 (1, 2, 1).

Row 2 P1 (1, 2, 1), [work row 2 of Panel Pattern, p0 (1, 2, 5), work row 2 of Orchid Chart, p0 (1, 2, 5)] 3 times, work row 2 of Panel Pattern, p1 (1, 2, 1).

Row 3 K1 (1, 2, 1), [work row 3 of Panel Pattern, k0 (1, 2, 5), work row 3 of Orchid Chart, k0 (1, 2, 5)] 3 times, work row 3 of Panel Pattern, k1 (1, 2, 1).

Row 4 P1 (1, 2, 1), [work row 4 of Panel Pattern, p0 (1, 2, 5), work row 4 of Orchid Chart, p0 (1, 2, 5)] 3 times, work row 4 of Panel Pattern, p1 (1, 2, 1).

Panel Pattern and Orchid Chart are now set.

Note To fit the orchid motif evenly up the length of the cardigan, work 16 (22, 4, 6) rows in stockinette stitch between the chart repeats, if desired.

Continue in Panel Pattern and Orchid Chart until the Back measures 14½ (15, 15½, 16)" (37 [38, 39.5, 40.5]cm) from the cast-on edge, ending with RS facing for next row.

ARMHOLE SHAPING

Bind off 6 (6, 6, 8) stitches at the beginning of the next 2 rows—81 (87, 95, 107) stitches.

Continue in pattern until the armhole measures 8 (8½, 9, 9½)" (20.5 [21.5, 23, 24]cm), ending with RS facing for next row.

SHOULDER SHAPING

Bind off 7 (8, 9, 10) stitches at the beginning of the next 4 rows, then 8 (9, 9, 11) stitches at the beginning of the following 2 rows. Leave the remaining 37 (37, 41, 45) stitches on a stitch holder.

Left Front

**With larger needles and MC, cast on 44 (44, 55, 66) stitches.

Work Edging Pattern once.

Knit 4 rows, increasing 1 (increasing 6, decreasing 1, decreasing 4) stitches evenly across the last row—45 (50, 54, 62) stitches.

Proceed as follows:

Row 1 K1 (2, 3, 6), work row 1 of Panel Pattern, k2 (3, 4, 5), work row 1 of Orchid Chart, k2 (3, 4, 5), work row 1 of Panel Pattern, k1 (3, 4, 7).

Row 2 P1 (3, 4, 7), work row 2 of Panel Pattern, p2 (3, 4, 5), work row 2 of Orchid Chart, p2 (3, 4, 5), work row 2 of Panel Pattern, p1 (2, 3, 6).

Row 3 K1 (2, 3, 6), work row 3 of Panel Pattern, k2 (3, 4, 5), work row 3 of Orchid Chart, k2 (3, 4, 5), work row 3 of Panel Pattern, k1 (3, 4, 7).

Row 4 P1 (3, 4, 7), work row 4 of Panel Pattern, p2 (3, 4, 5), work row 4 of Orchid Chart, p2 (3, 4, 5), work row 4 of Panel Pattern, p1 (2, 3, 6).

Panel Pattern and Chart are now set.

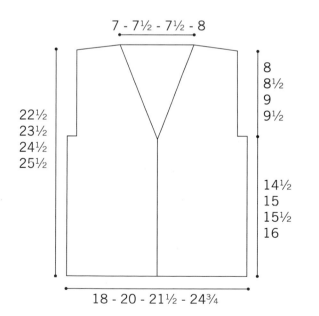

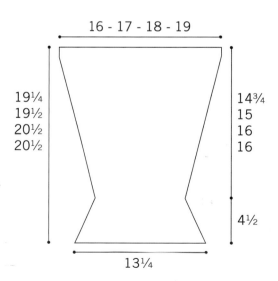

Note To fit the orchid motif evenly up the length of the cardigan, work 4 (6, 2, 10) rows in stockinette stitch between the
chart repeats, if desired.**

Continue in pattern until the Left Front measures 14½ (15,
15½, 16)" (37 [38, 39.5, 40.5]cm) from the cast-on edge,
ending with RS facing for next row.

NECKLINE AND ARMHOLE SHAPING

Next Row Bind off 6 (6, 6, 8) stitches, work to end. 39 (44,
48, 54) stitches.

Continuing in pattern, decrease 1 stitch at the neck edge on
the next and every alternate row to 28 (30, 32, 35) stitches,
then every 4th row to 22 (25, 27, 31) stitches.

Continue in pattern until the armhole measures 8 (8½, 9,
9½)" (20.5 [21.5, 23, 24]cm) and the last row of the Chart
has been worked, ending with RS facing for next row.

SHOULDER SHAPING

Bind off 7 (8, 9, 10) stitches at the beginning of the next 2
alternate rows. Work 1 row even in pattern. Bind off remaining 8 (9, 9, 11) stitches.

Right Front

Work from ** to ** as given for the Left Front.

Continue in pattern until the Right Front measures 14½ (15,
15½, 16)" (37 [38, 39.5, 40.5]cm) from the cast-on edge,
ending with WS facing for next row.

NECKLINE AND ARMHOLE SHAPING

Next Row Bind off 6 (6, 6, 8) stitches, work to end of row—
39 (44, 48, 54) stitches.

Continuing in pattern, decrease 1 stitch at the neck edge on
the next and every alternate row to 28 (30, 32, 35) stitches,
then every 4th row to 22 (25, 27, 31) stitches.

Continue in pattern until the armhole measures 8 (8½, 9,
9½)" (20.5 [21.5, 23, 24]cm) and the last row of the chart
has been worked, ending with WS facing for next row.

SHOULDER SHAPING

Bind off 7 (8, 9, 10) stitches at the beginning of the next 2
alternate rows. Work 1 row even in pattern. Bind off remaining 8 (9, 9, 11) stitches.

Sleeves (Make 2)

With larger needles and MC, cast on 66 stitches.

Work Edging Pattern once.

Knit 3 rows, decreasing 1 stitch at the center of the last row.
65 stitches.

Proceed as follows:

Row 1 (RS) K2, *work row 1 of Panel Pattern, k3; repeat
from * to last 2 stitches, k2.

Row 2 P2, *work row 2 of Panel Pattern, p3; repeat from * to
last 2 stitches, p2.

Continue as established; repeating Panel Pattern until the Sleeve measures 4½" (11.5cm) from the cast-on edge, ending with WS facing for next row.

Knit 3 rows.

Next row (RS) K3, *k2tog, k1; repeat from * to last 2 stitches, k2—45 stitches.

Foundation Row P16, work row 2 of Panel Pattern, p16.

Next Row K16, work row 1 of Panel Pattern, k16.

Next Row P16, work row 2 of Panel Pattern, p16.

Panel Pattern is now set.

Continue working Panel Pattern as established, increasing 1 stitch at each end of the needle on the 3rd and following 4th rows to 61 (73, 85, 96) stitches.

Size S, M, and L Only Increase 1 stitch at each end of the needle every 6th row to 81 (85, 91) stitches.

All sizes Continue in pattern until the Sleeve measures 19¼ (19½, 20½, 20½)" (49 [49.5, 52, 52]cm) from the cast-on edge, ending with RS facing for next row. Bind off.

Finishing

Pin all pieces to measurements and cover with a damp cloth. Leave the cloth to dry on the pieces.

Sew the shoulder seams. Sew in the Sleeves. Sew the side and Sleeve seams.

BUTTON AND BUTTONHOLE BAND

With RS of work facing, circular needle, and MC, pick up and knit 90 (94, 98, 102) stitches up Right Front, pick up and knit 41 (44, 46, 48) stitches up Right Front neck edge, knit 37 (37, 41, 45) stitches from back neck stitch holder, pick up and knit 41 (44, 46, 48) stitches down Left Front neck edge, and pick up and knit 90 (94, 98, 102) stitches down Left Front edge. 299 (313, 329, 345) stitches. Knit 1 row.

Next row (RS) K3, *yo, k2tog, k19 (20, 21, 22); repeat from * 3 times, k2tog, yo, knit to end—5 buttonholes made.

Knit 2 rows. Bind off knitwise.

Sew on the buttons, matching them to the buttonholes.

Intarsia

Some love it, others hate it. I have found that the ones who hate it leave the ends hanging to be woven in later. With practice, however, this can be done while you are knitting. As always, twist the yarns when changing color to prevent holes. The new color comes from underneath and over the current color and is worked. This twists the two colors together to prevent holes in work.

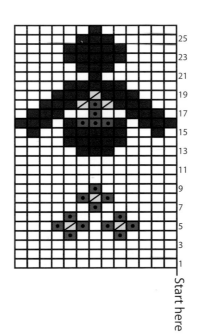

Key

◨ = A
◪ = B
■ = C

Start here

JUNE

FOR SUMMER KNITTING, think of projects that are quick and fun—ones that can be knit in the car while traveling or in front of the TV while watching movies at the cottage. The Adirondack Lap Blanket is just such a project, and it will be a comforting addition to your Adirondack chair (or Muskoka chair as its known in Canada) on those cool mornings when you're sipping coffee on the dock or patio. The Cottage Socks make great summer slippers, but are just as good for adding warmth to winter walks. Make them as stocking stuffers!

Don't forget that Father's Day falls in June, and while Dad may be happy with a pair of socks, why not knock his socks *off* with the Dad's Neighborhood Cardigan? The cables are only down the fronts, so easy summer knitting can continue!

 78  80  83

Laughter is the closest distance between two people.
—VICTOR BORGE
(1909–2000)

Adirondack Lap Blanket

This blanket is so soft, you will love the way it feels! The easy rib pattern features the introduction of a new color to expand your skills. Tassels are easy to make, and they add a bit of fun to the overall look. Keep your eye on this blanket: Someone will always be trying to grab it away from you when you're not looking!

Beginner

SIZE
34" x 42" (86.5cm x 106.5cm)

MATERIALS
Rowan Big Wool (3 oz
[100g]/87 yds [80m];
100% wool), (6) super bulky
  6 balls #35 Tremble (MC)
  1 ball #28 Bohemian (CC)

1 36" (90cm) US 17 (12mm)
circular needle or size required
to achieve gauge

1 tapestry needle

GAUGE
8 stitches and 10 rows = 4"
(10cm) in pattern

Needles

Don't let the term *circular needle* scare you! Think of a circular needle as two needles that just happen to be joined in the middle. These longer needles are great for working big projects like blankets. Instead of squishing all of the stitches onto straight needles and holding them up with sore arms, the circular needle allows you to rest the knitted work in your lap—and all the stitches fit!

Blanket

With MC, cast on 75 stitches.

Row 1 K5, *p5, k5; repeat from * to end.

Row 2 P5, *k5, p5; repeat from * to end.

Repeat rows 1–2 for ribbing.

Continue in ribbing until the Blanket measures 3" (7.5cm) from the cast-on edge, ending with RS facing for next row.

**Change to CC and work 2 rows in ribbing.

Change to MC and work 2 rows in ribbing.

Change to CC and work 2 rows in ribbing.**

Change to MC and continue in ribbing until the Blanket measures 37" (94cm) from the cast-on edge, ending with RS facing for next row.

Repeat from ** to **.

Change to MC and continue in ribbing for another 3" (7.5cm), ending with RS facing for next row. Bind off.

TASSELS (MAKE 4)

Cut a piece of cardboard into a 4" x 4" (10cm x 10cm) strip. Wind CC around cardboard 16 times. Break yarn, leaving a long end, and thread on a tapestry needle. Slip the needle through the loops and tie tightly. Wind the yarn 1" (2.5cm) below fold. Secure. Cut through the loops and trim evenly. Attach one tassel to each corner of the Blanket.

Cottage Socks

These socks are like slippers, worn slouched and cozy for around the home or cottage. They are also great at keeping toes warm during harsh wintery days.

SKILL LEVEL
Intermediate

SIZE
Child's Small (Child's Medium, Child's Large, Women's Small, Women's Medium, Women's Large, Men's Small, Men's Medium, Men's Large)

Length: 5½ (6½, 7, 8, 8½, 9, 9½, 10, 10½)" (14 [16.5, 18, 20.5, 21.5, 23, 24, 25.5, 26.5]cm)

MATERIALS
Classic Elite Yarns Montera (3½ oz [100g]/138 yds [126m]; 50% Llama/50% Wool), (4) medium
    Boy's: 1 hank each # 3821 Sage (MC), # 3823 Spring

Green (A), and # 3887 Pear (B)
Girl's: 1 hank #3819 Rose Quartz
Women's: 1 hank #3845 Fieldstone Heather
Men's: 1 hank #3848 Dye-pot Indigo

1 set of four US 8 (5mm) double-pointed needles

1 set of four US 9 (5.5mm) double-pointed needles or size required to achieve gauge

1 stitch holder

GAUGE
18 stitches and 30 rows = 4" (10cm) in stockinette stitch with larger needles

Note The instructions are written for the smallest size. When changes are necessary for larger sizes, those instructions are enclosed in parentheses.

Leg

BOY'S/MEN'S RIBBED SOCK VERSION ONLY

Boy's Small (Boy's Medium, Boy's Large, Men's Small, Men's Medium, Men's Large)

With larger needles and MC, cast on 28 (32, 36, 48, 52, 60) stitches. Divide on 3 needles as follows: 9-10-9 (11-10-11; 12-12-12; 16-16-16; 17-18-17; 20-20-20). Join to work in the round and place marker.

Next Rnd *K2, p2; repeat from * around.

Work in (k2, p2) ribbing for 2 (2, 2, 3, 3, 3)" (5 [5, 5, 7.5, 7.5, 7.5]cm).

Boys' Sizes Work 3 rows each with MC, A, and B, as pictured.

The last 9 rounds form the stripe pattern.

All Male Sizes Change to smaller needles and continue in ribbing (and the stripe pattern, for Boys' Version only) until the Sock measures 4½ (5½, 6½, 8, 8½, 9)" (11.5 [14.5, 16.5, 20.5, 21.5, 23]cm) from the cast-on edge.

Change to MC and proceed to Heel.

GIRL'S/WOMEN'S EDGED SOCK VERSION ONLY

Girl's Small (Girl's Medium, Girl's Large, Women's Small, Women's Medium, Women's Large)

With smaller needles, cast on 37 (42, 47, 52, 57, 62) stitches.

Work back and forth across needles in rows as follows:

Row 1 K1, yo, *(k5, sl 2nd, 3rd, 4th, and 5th stitches over the first stitch), yo; repeat from * to last stitch, k1—17 (19, 21, 23, 25, 27) stitches.

Row 2 P1, *(k1tbl, yon, p1) into next st, p1; repeat from * to end of row—33 (37, 41, 45, 49, 53) stitches.

Row 3 K1, k1tbl, *k3, k1tbl; repeat from * to last 3 stitches, k3.

Row 4 Knit, decreasing 5 stitches evenly across—28 (32, 36, 40, 44, 48) stitches.

Change to larger needles and join for working in the round. Work in stockinette stitch (knit every round) for 2 (2½, 3¼, 3½, 3¾, 3¾)" (5 [6.5, 8.25, 9, 9.5, 9.5]cm) Change to smaller needles and continue to knit in rounds until the Sock measures 4½ (5½, 6½, 7, 7½, 8)" (11.5 [14, 16.5, 18, 18, 20.5]cm) from the cast-on edge.

Heel

ALL SIZES

Next Row K7 (8, 9, 10, 11, 12, 12, 13, 15) stitches, turn.

Next Row P14 (16, 18, 20, 22, 24, 24, 26, 30). (This is to and past the marker.) Place the remaining 14 (16, 18, 20, 22, 24, 24, 26, 30) stitches on a stitch holder for the instep.

Continue on 14 (16, 18, 20, 22, 24, 24, 26, 30) heel stitches as follows:

Row 1 (RS) *Sl1p, k1; repeat from * to end of row.

Row 2 Sl1p, purl to end of row.

Repeat rows 1–2 for heel stitches 6 (7, 8, 9, 10, 11, 11, 12, 14) times.

SHAPE HEEL

Row 1 (RS) K9 (10, 11, 12, 13, 14, 14, 15, 17), ssk, k1, turn.

Row 2 Sl1p, p5, p2tog, p1, turn.

Row 3 Sl1p, knit to 1 stitch before gap, ssk, k1, turn.

Row 4 Sl1p, purl to 1 stitch before gap, p2tog, p1, turn.

Repeat rows 3–4 until all stitches have been worked (end p2tog), ending with RS facing for next round—10 (10, 12, 12, 14, 14, 14, 16, 18) heel stitches.

With RS facing and needle 1, pick up and knit 7 (8, 9, 10, 11, 12, 12, 13, 15) stitches along the left side of the heel. With needle 2, knit the 14 (16, 18, 20, 22, 24, 24, 26, 30) instep stitches from holder. With needle 3, pick up and knit 7 (8, 9, 10, 11, 12, 12, 13, 15) stitches along the right side of the heel—38 (42, 48, 52, 58, 62, 62, 68, 78) stitches.

With needle 3, knit 5 (5, 6, 6, 7, 7, 7, 8, 9). Beginning at center heel, work in rounds as follows:

Rnd 1 Needle 1: Knit to last 3 stitches, k2tog, k1. Needle 2: Knit. Needle 3: K1, ssk, knit to end.

Rnd 2 Knit.

Repeat rounds 1–2 until there are 28 (32, 36, 40, 44, 48, 48, 52, 60) stitches remaining.

Work even in stockinette stitch until foot measures 4½ (5½, 6½, 7½, 8, 8, 8½, 9, 9½)" (11.5 [14, 16.5, 19, 20.5, 20.5, 21.5, 23, 24]cm) from picked up stitches at heel.

Toe

Rnd 1 Needle 1: Knit to last 3 stitches, k2tog, k1. Needle 2: K1, ssk, knit to last 3 stitches, k2tog, k1. Needle 3: K1, ssk, knit to end.

Rnd 2 Knit.

Repeat rounds 1–2 until there are 16 (16, 16, 20, 20, 24, 24, 28, 32) stitches remaining.

Repeat round 1 until there are 8 stitches remaining (6 stitches for Child's Small).

Graft the stitches together (page 140). Weave in loose end.

Knitting with Double-Pointed Needles

There are two things to remember when knitting with double-pointed needles (not to be confused with circular needles). One is to not twist the stitches when casting on. Once you have distributed the stitches evenly on 3 needles and before you begin your first round, check that all the stitches are lined up along the needles and that the yarn is at the back.

Dad's Neighborhood Cardigan

Cardigans look great on guys whether for comfort or fashion, and the zipper keeps it looking sporty and modern.

Experienced

SIZE

Small (Medium, Large, X-Large)

Chest: 34–36 (38–40, 42–44, 46–48)" (86–91 [97–102, 107–112, 117–122]cm)

Finished chest: 39 (44, 47, 51)" (99 [109, 119.5, 129.5]cm)

MATERIALS

8 (8, 9, 10) balls Patons Classic Merino Wool (3 oz [100g]/223 yds [204m]; 100% merino wool) #224 Gray Mix, **3** light

1 pair US 6 (4mm) needles

1 pair US 7 (4.5mm) needles or size required to obtain gauge

1 36" (90cm) US 6 (4mm) circular needle

1 cable needle

3 stitch holders

16 (16, 18, 18)" (40.5 [40.5, 45.5, 45.5]cm) separating zipper

GAUGE

20 stitches and 26 rows = 4" (10cm) in stockinette stitch with larger needles

STITCH PATTERNS

REVERSE BROKEN RIB STITCH

Row 1 (RS): Purl.

Row 2: Knit.

Row 3: P2, *k2, p2; repeat from * to end of row.

Row 4: K2, *p2, k2; repeat from * to end of row.

Repeat rows 1–4 for Pattern Stitch.

CABLE PATTERN

Row 1: K6, t5r, p1, c2l, p1, t5l, k6.

Row 2 and All WS Rows: Knit the knit stitches and purl the purl stitches.

Row 3: K5, t5r, p2, c2l, p2, t5l, k5.

Row 5: K4, t5r, p3, c2l, p3, t5l, k4.

Row 7: K3, t5r, p4, c2l, p4, t5l, k3.

Row 9: K2, t5r, p5, c2l, p5, t5l, k2.

Row 11: K1, t5r, p6, c2l, p6, t5l, k1.

Row 13: T5r, p7, c2l, p7, t5l.

Row 15: C5l, p7, c2l, p7, c5r.

Row 17: K1, c5l, p6, c2l, p6, c5r, k1.

Row 19: K2, c5l, p5, c2l, p5, c5r, k2.

Row 21: K3, c5l, p4, c2l, p4, c5r, k3.

Row 23: K4, c5l, p3, c2l, p3, c5r, k4.

Row 25: K5, c5l, p2, c2l, p2, c5r, k5.

Row 27: K6, c5l, p1, c2l, p1, c5r, k6.

Row 28: Knit the knit stitches and purl the purl stitches.

Repeat rows 1–28 for Cable Pattern.

Note The instructions are written for the smallest size. When changes are necessary for larger sizes, those instructions are enclosed in parentheses.

Back

With smaller needles, cast on 109 (121, 133, 143) stitches.

Row 1 K1, *p1, k1; repeat from * to end of row.

Row 2 P1, *k1, p1; repeat from * to end of row.

Repeat rows 1–2 for seed stitch. Work in seed stitch for 1¼" (3cm) ending with RS facing for next row and increasing 9 (9, 9, 11) stitches evenly across the last row—118 (130, 142, 154) stitches.

Change to larger needles and work in Pattern Stitch until the

Back measures 16 (16, 18, 18)" (40.5 [40.5, 45.5, 45.5]cm) from the cast-on edge, ending with RS facing for next row.

ARMHOLE SHAPING

Bind off 5 (7, 7, 7) stitches at the beginning of the next 2 rows—108 (116, 128, 140) stitches.

Continue even in pattern until the armhole measures 9½ (10, 10½, 11)" (24 [25.5, 26.5, 28]cm), ending with RS facing for next row.

SHOULDER SHAPING

Bind off 11 (12, 14, 15) stitches at the beginning of the next 4 rows, then 12 (12, 14, 16) stitches at the beginning of the next 2 rows. Leave the remaining 40 (44, 44, 48) stitches on stitch holder.

Left Front

**With smaller needles, cast on 55 (61, 67, 71) stitches.

Work in seed stitch as given for the Back for 1¼" (3cm), ending with RS facing for next row and increasing 5 stitches evenly across the last row—60 (66, 72, 76) stitches.**

Change to larger needles and proceed as follows:

Row 1 Work 24 (30, 36, 40) stitches in Pattern Stitch. Work row 1 of Cable Pattern. Work in Pattern Stitch to end.

Row 2 Work 10 stitches in Pattern Stitch. Work Row 2 of Cable Pattern. Work in Pattern Stitch to end.

Cable Pattern is now set. Continue as established until the Left Front measures 16 (16, 18, 18)" (40.5 [40.5, 45.5, 45.5]cm) from the cast-on edge, ending with RS facing for next row.

ARMHOLE AND NECK SHAPING

Next Row Bind off 5 (7, 7, 7) stitches, work to end of row—55 (59, 65, 69) stitches. Work 1 row even.

Continuing in Cable Pattern, decrease 1 stitch at the neck edge on the next and every following row to 45 (55, 56, 60) stitches, then every alternate row to 34 (36, 42, 46) stitches.

Continue even until armhole measures 9½ (10, 10½, 11)" (24 [25.5, 26.5, 28]cm), ending with RS facing for next row.

SHOULDER SHAPING

Bind off 11 (12, 14, 15) stitches at the beginning of the next and following alternate row. Work 1 row even. Bind off remaining 12 (12, 14, 16) stitches.

Right Front

Work from ** to ** as given for Left Front.

Change to larger needles and proceed as follows:

Row 1 Work 10 stitches in Reverse Broken Rib Stitch. Work row 1 of Cable Pattern. Work Reverse Broken Rib Stitch to end.

Row 2 Work 24 (30, 36, 40) stitches in Reverse Broken Rib Stitch. Work row 2 of Cable Pattern. Work Reverse Broken Rib Stitch to end.

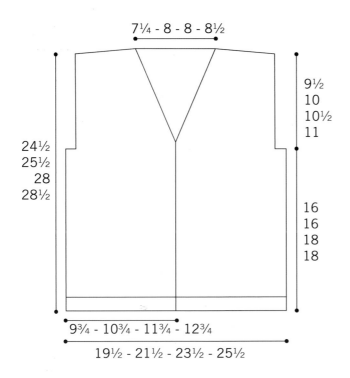

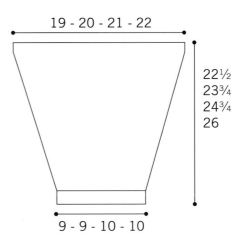

Cable Pattern is now set. Continue as established until the Right Front measures 16 (16, 18, 18)" (40.5 [40.5, 45.5, 45.5]cm) from the cast-on edge, ending with WS facing for next row.

ARMHOLE AND NECK SHAPING

Next Row Bind off 5 (7, 7, 7) stitches, work to end. 55 (59, 65, 69) stitches.

Continuing in Cable Pattern, decrease 1 stitch at the neck edge on the next and every following 4th row to 45 (55, 56, 60) stitches, then every 2nd row to 34 (36, 42, 46) stitches.

Continue even until the armhole measures 9½ (10, 10½, 11)" (24 [25.5, 26.5, 28]cm) from the cast-on edge, ending with WS facing for next row.

SHOULDER SHAPING

Bind off 11 (12, 14, 15) stitches at the beginning of the next and following alternate row. Work 1 row even. Bind off remaining 12 (12, 14, 16) stitches.

Sleeves (Make 2)

With smaller needles, cast on 51 (51, 57, 57) stitches.

Work in seed stitch as given for the Back for 1¼" (3cm), ending with RS facing for next row.

Change to larger needles and proceed in pattern as given for Back, AT THE SAME TIME increase 1 stitch at each end of the needle on the 3rd and following 4th row to 95 (99, 95, 99) stitches, and every following 6th row to 115 (121, 127, 133) stitches, taking increased stitches into pattern. Continue even until the Sleeve measures 22½ (23¾, 24¾, 26)" (57 [60.5, 63, 66]cm) from the cast-on edge, ending with RS facing for next row. Bind off.

Finishing

Pin all pieces to measurements and cover with a damp cloth. Leave the cloth to dry on the pieces.

Sew the shoulder seams.

With RS of work facing and circular needle: Pick up and knit 84 (84, 96, 96) stitches up Right Front edge. Pick up and knit 49 (54, 56, 58) stitches up the Right Front neck edge. Knit 40 (44, 44, 48) from the Back neck stitch holder. Pick up and knit 49 (54, 56, 58) stitches down the Left Front neck edge. Pick up and knit 84 (84, 96, 96) stitches down the Left Front edge—302 (316, 344, 350) stitches.

Knit 2 rows. Bind off knitwise (WS).

Pin the zipper and sew it into place under the edge.

Sew in the Sleeves. Sew the side and Sleeve seams.

Zippers

To sew in zippers, first pin the zipper into place so that the edges of the knitting meet at the center and cover the teeth of the zipper. Baste the zipper into place. With WS facing, whipstitch (page 65) the edge of the zipper into place, then backstitch close to the teeth to finish.

BACK STITCH

JULY

JULY IS THE "YAHOO!" kick-up-your-heels month. School is officially out, and the summer holidays have begun in earnest. Remember when summers lasted forever when you were a child? You may have the summer off with your children, or be off from school yourself. Or you may take your vacation in July. In any case, July is a time you can escape your "real" life and recapture those childhood summer days. Drive to the nearest beach with your picnic. Collect the books you want to spend lazy hours reading. Find the quiet and solitude you deserve.

Above all, July is a perfect knitting month. The long drives to the country, visiting relatives or friends, or the extra vacation time are ideal for bringing out two sticks and some string. Knitting on a dock by the water can make for an enjoyable afternoon.

Whatever you are by nature, keep to it; never desert your line of talent. Be what nature intended you for, and you will succeed.
—SYDNEY SMITH (1771–1845)

89

91

94

Cottage Table Settings

Dressed up or down, these table settings are as versatile as they are practical. They are totally washable in cotton and have a wonderful, earthy look. Enlist a kid to help. My daughter put on the beads. Coordinate the yarn and beads with the color of your own plates or furniture.

Beginner

SIZE
Place Mats: 16" x 10" (40.5cm x 25.5cm)

Table Runner: 46" x 14" (117cm x 35.5cm)

MATERIALS
Lily Sugar N' Cream (2½ oz [70g]/120 yds [109m]; 100% cotton), (4) medium
   6 balls #00082 Jute (MC)
   1 ball #00001 White (A)
   1 ball #00003 Cream (B)

1 pair US 7 (4.5mm) needles or size required to achieve gauge

1 36" (90cm) US 7 (4.5mm) circular needle

382 beads or desired amount (Note: Ensure the yarn will fit through the bead opening)

1 US H-8 (5mm) crochet hook

GAUGE
20 stitches and 26 rows = 4" (10cm) in stockinette stitch

COLORWORK
STRIPE PATTERN

Work 1 row in A.
Work 2 rows in MC.
Work 2 rows in B.
Work 1 row in A.
Work 2 rows in B.
Work 2 rows in MC.
Work 1 row in A.
Work 2 rows in MC.

Place Mat (make 4)

Note Place mat is worked sideways.

With MC, cast on 35 stitches.

Row 1 (RS) K1, *p1, k1; repeat from * to end of row.

Repeat this row 6 times more for seed stitch.

Next row (WS) Purl, increasing 5 stitches evenly across— 40 stitches.

Work 4 rows in stockinette stitch.

Work 12 rows of Stripe Pattern in stockinette stitch.

With MC, work in stockinette stitch until the Place Mat measures 12" (30cm) from the cast-on edge, ending with RS facing for next row.

Work 12 rows of Stripe Pattern in stockinette stitch.

With MC, work 5 rows in stockinette stitch.

Next Row (WS) Purl, decreasing 5 stitches evenly across— 35 stitches.

Work 8 rows in seed stitch. Bind off all stitches.

BORDER
With MC, pick up and knit 69 stitches along the top edge. Work in seed stitch for 8 rows. Bind off in seed stitch. Repeat for the bottom border.

Table Runner

With MC, cast on 53 stitches.

Row 1 (RS) K1, *p1, k1; repeat from * to end of row.

Repeat this row 6 times more for seed stitch.

Next row (WS) Purl, increasing 7 stitches evenly across— 60 stitches.

Work 4 rows in stockinette stitch.

Proceed in stockinette stitch as follows:

***Work 12 rows of Stripe Pattern.

With MC, work 2" (5cm) in stockinette stitch, ending with RS facing for next row.

Work 12 rows of Stripe Pattern.***

With MC, work stockinette stitch until the Table Runner measures 40" (101.5cm) from the cast-on edge, ending with RS facing for next row.

Repeat from *** to *** once.

With MC, work 5 rows stockinette stitch.

Next row (WS) Purl, decreasing 7 stitches evenly across—53 stitches.

Work 8 rows in seed stitch. Bind off all stitches.

BORDER

With MC, pick up and knit 169 stitches along one side edge. Work in seed stitch for 8 rows. Bind off in seed stitch. Repeat for the other side.

Bead Fringe

Cut a strand of MC 7" (17.75cm) long. Fold in half. With crochet hook, pull folded end of strand through the short edge of the Place Mats and Table Runner from front to back, every ½" (1cm). Slip end through loop before pulling tight. Repeat along edges until you have the desired amount of fringe. Thread beads onto random strands and knot into place. Repeat on the other side of each Place Mat and Table Runner. Trim evenly.

Beading

There is a wonderful array of beads out there that will certainly stir your creative juices. But be careful to ensure your yarn will fit through the holes of the beads. Cut a strand of your yarn and take it with you when you go bead shopping to check. I use a needle threader with a size 18 needlepoint needle to thread the beads on the yarn.

Rosseau Bandeau

Filled with beautiful lakes, Ontario is a popular place for vacationing at summer cottages. Lake Rosseau is one such lake; it inspires lounging on the dock, slowing life down, and taking in nature with some cool shades and a cute bikini.

Intermediate

SIZE
X-Small (Small, Medium, Large)

Bust: 28 (30–32, 34–36, 38–40)" (71 [76–81.5, 86.5–91.5, 96.5–101.5]cm)

Finished size: 29 (32, 34, 38)" (73.5 [81.25, 86.5, 96.5]cm)
Bottom:One Size

MATERIALS
Butterfly Super 10 (4½ oz [125g]/250 yds [228m]; 100% mercerized cotton), (4) medium

1 skein each of #3947 Violet (MC), #3062 Azure (A), #3784 Imperial Teal (B)

1 pair US 7 (4.5mm) needles or size required to achieve gauge

1 US G-6 (4mm) crochet hook

4 stitch holders

60" (152.5cm) length skin-toned elastic, ⅖" (1cm) wide.

GAUGE
20 stitches and 26 rows = 4" (10cm) in stockinette stitch

Note The instructions are written for the smallest size. When changes are necessary for larger sizes, those instructions are enclosed in parentheses.

Front

**With MC, cast on 74 (82, 86, 90) stitches.

Row 1 (RS) P2, *k2, p2; repeat from * to end of row.

Row 2 K2, *p2, k2; repeat from * to end of row.

Repeat rows 1–2 for ribbing. Work 8 rows more in (k2, p2) ribbing.

Knit 1 row.**

***Change to A and work 4 rows in stockinette stitch.

Change to B and work 4 rows in stockinette stitch.

Change to MC and work 4 rows in stockinette stitch.***

Work from *** to *** once (once, twice, twice) more.

Change to A. Purl 1 row.

With A, work 10 rows in (k2, p2) ribbing. Bind off in ribbing.

Back

Work from ** to ** as given for Front.

Work from *** to *** as given for Front once, AT THE SAME TIME increase 1 stitch at each end of the needle on the 3rd and following alternate rows twice—80 (88, 92, 96) stitches.

Next Row With B, k24 (25, 25, 27), turn. Place remaining stitches on first stitch holder.

Next Row Purl.

Next Row Knit to last 2 stitches, k2tog.

Next Row Change to MC, p2tog, purl to end.

Continue to work in stripes as given above, continuing to decrease 1 stitch at the back opening every row to 8 stitches. Place remaining stitches on second stitch holder.

With RS facing, place next 32 (38, 42, 42) stitches from first stitch holder onto a third stitch holder.

Next Row Join B to remaining stitches and proceed as follows:

Row 1 (RS) K2tog, knit to end.

Row 2 Purl to last 2 stitches, p2tog.

Continue in Stripe Pattern, continuing to decrease 1 stitch at the back opening every row to 8 stitches. Place remaining stitches on a fourth stitch holder.

Finishing

With RS facing and B, knit 8 stitches from the second stitch holder. Pick up and knit 16 stitches down right back opening. Knit across 32 (38, 42, 42) stitches from the third stitch holder, decreasing 2 (0, 0, 0) stitches evenly across. Pick up and knit 16 stitches up left back opening. Knit 8 stitches from the fourth stitch holder—78 (86, 90, 90) stitches. Work in (k2, p2) ribbing as given for Front for 8 rows. Bind off in ribbing.

Sew the sides. Fold the ribbing at bottom in half and sew the edge down using whipstitch (page 65), creating an opening for the elastic. Insert the elastic, pulling to a comfortable fit. Sew the ends of the elastic together and then sew the opening closed. Repeat for the top ribbing.

Bottom

With A, cast on 41 stitches.

Row 1 (RS) K1, sl1, k1, psso, *yo, k2tog; repeat from * to last 2 stitches, k2tog. 39 stitches.

Row 2 Purl.

Repeat rows 1–2 four times more. 31 stitches.

Begin working in stockinette stitch, continuing to decrease 1 stitch at each end of the needle as in row 1 on the next and every alternate row until there are 15 stitches remaining.

Work even in stockinette stitch for 5" (12.5cm), ending with RS facing for next row.

Increase 1 stitch at each end of the needle on every row until there are 61 stitches. Work even in stockinette stitch until the Bottom measures 17½" (44.5cm) from the cast-on edge, ending with RS facing for next row. Bind off, leaving the last stitch on the needle.

Slip the remaining stitch onto the crochet hook. Ch 3, work 62 hdc along the first side edge, ch 3 at corner, work 31 hdc across the top front edge, ch 3 at corner, work 62 hdc along second side edge, ch 3 at corner, work 40 hdc across the top back edge, sl st to 2nd ch of first ch 3, work chain st 15½" (39.5cm) long for Strap. Fasten off.

Sl st to next corner ch-3 sp of front. Make a chain 15½" (39.5cm) long for strap. Fasten off.

Repeat for 2 remaining corners.

Finishing

Sew elastic thread along each side of the leg openings. Optional: Sew swimsuit lining into crotch using a ¼" (6mm) seam allowance.

Swimwear

The bathing suits in this book (the Rosseau Bandeau here and the BVI Bikini, page 43) are for landlubbers only. Cotton will absorb water and sag, so it is not meant for athletic endeavors in the water. I don't want to give you the impression that the elastic will keep it all together while wet: It may not. It is there to keep the sides and body bits in! If you want something to swim in, you may want to experiment with manmade fibers, which keep their shape when wet. The Rosseau Bandeau and BVI Bikini are best for catching rays.

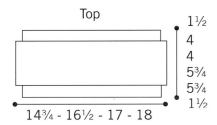

Top

1½
4
4
5¾
5¾
1½

14¾ - 16½ - 17 - 18

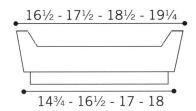

16½ - 17½ - 18½ - 19¼

14¾ - 16½ - 17 - 18

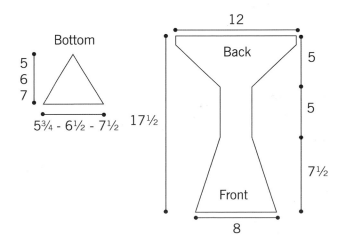

Bottom

5
6
7

5¾ - 6½ - 7½

17½

12

Back

5

5

7½

Front

8

Boat Launch Cables

When I picked up the test knitter's finished Boat Launch Cables, the test knitter, Alina, said, "This is a Joanne sweater." I immediately threw it on and loved it. My niece, Sarah, who models it here, gushed, "Oooh, this is nice!" Then after sending the photos for the book to my agent, Marlene, for her feedback, this was the sweater she said she wanted to knit. It seems to have something for everyone.

Experienced

SIZE
Small (Medium, Large, X-Large)

Bust: 30–32 (34–36, 38–40, 42–44)" (76–81.5 [86.5–91.5, 96.5–101.5, 106.5–112]cm)

Finished size: 33 (38, 42, 48)" (84 [96.5, 106.5, 122]cm)

MATERIALS
12 (13, 14, 15) balls Classic Elite Yarns Bamboo (1¾ oz [50g]/77 yds [70m]; 100% bamboo) #4916 Natural, (3) light

1 pair US 6 (4mm) needles

1 pair US 7 (4.5mm) needles or size required to achieve gauge

2 US 6 (4mm) double-pointed needles

1 cable needle

1 stitch holder

GAUGE
20 stitches and 26 rows = 4" (10cm) in stockinette stitch

STITCH PATTERNS
DOUBLE WAVES PATTERN

Row 1 (RS): K2, p3, k2, p2, k2, p3, k2.
Row 2 and All WS Rows: Knit all knit stitches and purl all purl stitches.
Row 3: T3f, p2, t3f, t3b, p2, t3b.
Row 5: P1, t3f, p2, c4f, p2, t3b, p1.
Row 7: P2, (t3f, t3b) twice, p2.

Row 9: P3, c4f, p2, c4f, p3.
Row 11: P2, (t3b, t3f) twice, p2.
Row 13: P1, t3b, p2, c4f, p2, t3f, p1.
Row 15: T3b, p2, t3b, t3f, p2, t3f.
Row 17: As for row 1.
Row 19: As for row 3.
Row 21: P1, t3f, p2, c4b, p2, t3b, p1.
Row 23: As for row 7.
Row 25: P3, c4b, p2, c4b, p3.
Row 27: As for row 11.
Row 29: P1, t3b, p2, c4b, p2, t3f, p1.
Row 31: As for row 15.
Row 32: As for row 2.
Repeat rows 1–32 for Double Waves Pattern.

SNAKE CABLE PATTERN

Row 1 (RS): K6.
Rows 2 and All WS Rows: Purl.
Row 3: C6b.
Rows 5–8: Repeat rows 1–2 twice.
Row 9: C6f.
Rows 11–12: Repeat rows 1–2.
Repeat rows 1–12 for Snake Cable Pattern.

"O" PATTERN

Row 1 (RS): C2b, c2f.
Row 2 and All WS Rows: Purl
Row 3: C2f, c2b.
Repeat rows 1–4 for "O" Pattern.

Note The instructions are written for the smallest size. When changes are necessary for larger sizes, those instructions are enclosed in parentheses.

Right Front
**With smaller needles, cast on 70 (76, 82, 90) stitches.

Row 1 (RS) *K1, p1; repeat from * to end of row.

Row 2 *P1, k1; repeat from * to end of row.

Repeat rows 1–2 for seed stitch for 1½" (4cm), ending with RS facing for next row and increasing 13 (14, 15, 14) stitches evenly across the last row—83 (90, 97, 104) stitches.**

Change to larger needles and proceed as follows:

Row 1 P2, work row 1 of Double Waves Pattern, p2, k3, p2, work row 1 of "O" Pattern, p2, k3, p2, work row 1 of Snake Cable Pattern, p2, k3, p2, work row 1 of "O" Pattern, p2, k3,

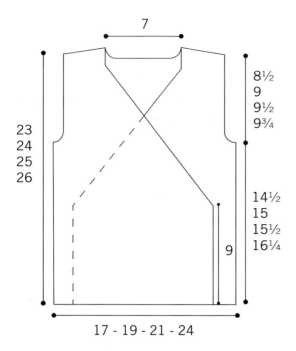

needle on the next and every following alternate row 3 (4, 6, 10) times—47 (53, 56, 57) stitches.

Continuing in pattern, decrease 1 stitch at the front edge on every 2nd row to 20 (25, 26, 27) stitches.

Continue even until the armhole measures 8½ (9, 9½, 9¾)" (21.5 [23, 23.5, 25]cm), ending with WS facing for next row.

SHOULDER SHAPING

Bind off 7 (8, 8, 8) stitches on the next and following alternate row. Work 1 row even. Bind off the remaining stitches.

p2, work row 1 of Double Waves Pattern, (p2, k3, p2) 1 (2, 3, 4) time(s).

Row 2 Knit all knit stitches and purl all purl stitches.

Row 3 P2, work row 3 of Double Waves Pattern, p2, k3, p2, work row 3 of "O" Pattern, p2, k3, p2, work row 3 of Snake Cable Pattern, p2, k3, p2, work row 3 of "O" Pattern, p2, k3, p2, work row 3 of Double Waves Pattern, (p2, k3, p2) 1 (2, 3, 4) time(s).

Row 4 As row 2.

Pattern is now set.

Continue in pattern until the Right Front measures 9" (23cm) from the cast-on edge, ending with RS facing for next row.

NECK SHAPING

Decrease 1 stitch at the front edge on the next 23 (17, 11, 5) rows, then every 2nd row 6 (11, 15, 21) times—54 (62, 71, 78) stitches.

ARMHOLE SHAPING

Next row (WS): Bind off 3 (4, 8, 10) stitches. Work in pattern to end of row.

Continuing in pattern, decrease 1 stitch at each end of the

Left Front

Work from ** to ** as given for the Right Front.

Change to larger needles and proceed as follows:

Row 1 (RS) (P2, k3, p2) 1 (2, 3, 4) times, work row 1 of Double Waves Pattern, p2, k3, p2, work row 1 of "O" Pattern, p2, k3, p2, work row 1 of Snake Cable Pattern, p2, k3, p2, work row 1 of "O" Pattern, p2, k3, p2, work row 1 of Double Waves Pattern, p2.

Row 2 Knit all knit stitches and purl all purl stitches as they appear.

Row 3 (P2, k3, p2) 1 (2, 3, 4) time(s), work row 3 of Double Waves Pattern, p2, k3, p2, work row 3 of "O" Pattern, p2, k3, p2, work row 3 of Snake Cable Pattern, p2, k3, p2, work row 3 of "O" Pattern, p2, k3, p2, work row 3 of Double Waves Pattern, p2.

Row 4 As for row 2.

Pattern is now set.

Continue in pattern until the Left Front measures 9" (23cm) from the cast-on edge, ending with WS facing for next row.

NECK SHAPING

Decrease 1 stitch at the front edge on the next 23 (17, 11, 5) rows, then every 2nd row 6 (11, 15, 21) times—54 (62, 71, 78) stitches.

ARMHOLE SHAPING

Next row (RS): Bind off 3 (4, 8, 10) stitches, work in pattern to last 2 stitches, k2tog.

Continuing in pattern, decrease 1 stitch at each end of the needle on the next and every 2nd row 3 (4, 6, 10) times—47 (53, 56, 57) stitches.

Continuing in pattern, decrease 1 stitch at the neck edge on every 2nd row to 20 (25, 26, 27) stitches.

Continue even until the armhole measures 8½ (9, 9½, 9¾)" (21.5 [23, 23.5, 25]cm), ending with RS facing for next row.

SHOULDER SHAPING

Bind off 7 (8, 8, 8) stitches on the next and following alternate row. Work 1 row even. Bind off remaining stitches.

Back

With smaller needles, cast on 74 (84, 96, 110) stitches.

Work in seed stitch as given for the Right Front for 1½" (4cm), ending with RS facing for next row and increasing 14 (18, 20, 20) stitches evenly across the last row—88 (102, 116, 130) stitches.

Change to larger needles and proceed as follows:

Row 1 (RS) (P2, k3, p2) 1 (2, 3, 4) time(s), work row 1 of Double Waves Pattern, p2, k3, p2, work row 1 of "O" Pattern, p2, k3, p2, work row 1 of Snake Cable Pattern, p2, k3, p2, work row 1 of "O" Pattern, p2, k3, p2, work row 1 of Double Waves Pattern, (p2, k3, p2,) 1 (2, 3, 4) time(s).

Row 2 Knit all knit stitches and purl all purl stitches as they appear.

Row 3 (P2, k3, p2,) 1 (2, 3, 4) time(s), work row 3 of Double Waves Pattern, p2, k3, p2, work row 3 of "O" Pattern, p2, k3, p2, work row 3 of Snake Cable Pattern, p2, k3, p2, work row 3 of "O" Pattern, p2, k3, p2, work row 3 of Double Waves Pattern, (p2, k3, p2,) 1 (2, 3, 4) time(s).

Row 4 As for row 2.

Pattern is now set.

Continue in pattern until the Back measures the same length as the Fronts before armhole, ending with RS facing for next row.

ARMHOLE SHAPING

Bind off 3 (4, 8, 10) stitches at the beginning of the next 2 rows—82 (94, 100, 110) stitches.

Continuing in pattern, decrease 1 stitch at each end of the needle on the next and every following alternate row 3 (4, 6, 10) times—74 (84, 86, 88) stitches.

Continue even until the armhole measures 8½ (9, 9½, 9¾)" (21.5 [23, 23.5, 25]cm), ending with RS facing for next row.

SHOULDER SHAPING (LEFT SIDE)

Next Row Bind off 7 (8, 8, 8) stitches, work in pattern 16 (21, 21, 22) stitches (including stitch after bind off), turn. Leave the remaining stitches on spare needle.

Next Row P2tog, work in pattern to end of row.

Next Row Bind off 7 (8, 8, 8) stitches, work in pattern to last 2 stitches, k2tog.

Next Row P2tog, work in pattern to end of row.

Bind off remaining 6 (9, 10, 11) stitches.

SHOULDER SHAPING (RIGHT SIDE)

With RS facing, slip next 28 stitches from spare needle onto stitch holder for the Back Neck. Continue with spare needle and pattern to end.

Next row (WS) Bind off 7 (8, 8, 8) stitches, work in pattern to last 2 stitches, p2tog.

Next Row K2tog, work in pattern to end of row.

Decreasing with Cables

You may find that your cable is interrupted when you decrease stitches. First, you may want to consider whether the interrupted cable will be hidden by the "wrapped over" part of the sweater. If not, you will want to have the neatest edge possible (you may want to even if the edge is hidden). If, for instance, you are working a C6B, you could cable 3 over 2 stitches (rather than 3 stitches), thereby decreasing the last stitch of the 3 held at the back (not on the cable needle). Otherwise, you can omit the cable and work in stockinette stitch for the decrease.

Next Row Bind off 7 (8, 8, 8) stitches, work in pattern to last 2 stitches, p2tog.

Bind off remaining 6 (9, 10, 11) stitches.

Finishing

Block the pieces to the measurements. Sew the shoulder seams.

With smaller needles and RS facing, pick up and knit 36 stitches up Right Front edge, 71 (75, 79, 81) stitches up Right Front neck edge. Knit 28 stitches across Back neck edge, decreasing 9 stitches evenly across (19 stitches). Pick up and knit 71 (75, 79, 81) stitches down Left Front neck edge, and 36 stitches down Left Front edge—233 (241, 249, 253) stitches.

Work in seed stitch for 4 rows. Bind off all stitches.

With smaller needles and RS facing, pick up and knit 68 (72, 76, 78) stitches along armhole edge.

Work in seed stitch for 4 rows. Bind off.

Sew the side seams.

TIES (MAKE 2)

With set of 2 double-pointed needles, cast on 4 stitches.

Row 1 *Knit, slide stitches to end of the needle, do not turn.

Row 2 Knit, pulling yarn across back tightly. Repeat from * until I-cord measures 7" (17.75cm). Thread yarn through all stitches and pull tightly. Attach to side.

Note: For inside ties, simply tie on a single strand of yarn to prevent bulk.

AUGUST

I HAVE MIXED FEELINGS about August. The days are long and lazy, but nagging in the back of my head is that autumn is peeking around the corner. Sumptuous fashions have hit the stores, and new yarn is spilling out of your LYS (local yarn shop). I try not to notice while I still walk around in my bathing suit and flip-flops. Fall brings with it a quicker pace, schedules, deadlines, driving to practices and lessons. August pulls us back to its lazy morning sun, streaming through lacy bedroom drapes, and coffee on the sunny back porch. Breakfast near lunchtime, lunch becomes a snack, and dinner consists of BBQs laden with grilled yummies.

Knitting lace has similar qualities. It can be scheduled and tedious, but it can also have the ease and lightness of August. Airy mohair and easy purling on the wrong sides make for the perfect late-summer project. My mind likes to wander while I knit—easy to do on the purl rows. The slow pace of an August day prolongs the inevitable end of summer. Savor it.

If you want others to be happy, practice compassion. If you want to be happy, practice compassion.
—THE DALAI LAMA (1935—)

 102

 105

 107

Lace Pillows

The airy, ethereal look of kid mohair produces forces me to suppress the urge to knit curtains with it. It is so lovely! But pay attention to your pattern. The loveliness will fade if you have to rip out stitches!

Beginner

SIZE

16" x 16" (40.5cm x 40.5cm)

MATERIALS

Crystal Palace Kid Merino 1 oz [25g]/240 yds [219m]; 28% Kid Mohair/28% Merino Wool/44% Micro Nylon), **(3)** light

3 balls Apple (A)

3 balls Pink (B)

1 pair US 6 (4mm) needles or size required to achieve gauge

Two 16" x 16" (40.5cm x 40.5cm) pillow inserts

GAUGE

21 stitches and 24 rows = 4" (10cm) in Pattern A.

21 stitches and 30 rows = 4" (10cm) in Pattern B.

STITCH PATTERNS

PATTERN A

Row 1 and All WS Rows (WS): Purl.

Row 2: K2, *k1, yo, ssk, k1, k2tog, yo; repeat from * to last 3 stitches, k3.

Row 4: K4, *yo, k3; repeat from * to last stitch, k1.

Row 6: K2, k2tog, *yo, ssk, k1, k2tog, yo, sl2 knitwise, k1, p2sso; repeat from * to last 4 stitches, ending yo, ssk, k2.

Row 8: K2, *k1, k2tog, yo, k1, yo, ssk; repeat from * to last 3 stitches, k3.

Row 10: As for row 4.

Row 12: K2, *k1, k2tog, yo, sl2 knitwise, k1, p2sso, yo, ssk; repeat from * to last 3 stitches, k3.

Repeat rows 1–12 for Pattern A.

PATTERN B

Row 1 and All WS Rows (WS): Purl.

Row 2: K4, * yo, ssk, k1, (k2tog, yo) twice, k3; repeat from * to end.

Row 4: *K3, (yo, ssk) twice, k1, k2tog, yo; repeat from * to last 4 stitches, k4.

Row 6: K2, *(yo, ssk) 3 times, k4; repeat from * to last 2 stitches, yo, ssk.

Row 8: K1, *(yo, ssk) 4 times, k2; repeat from * to last 3 stitches, yo, ssk, k1.

Rows 10, 12 & 14: As rows 6, 4 & 2.

Row 16: K2tog, yo *k4, (k2tog, yo) 3 times; repeat from * to last 2 stitches, k2.

Row 18: K1, k2tog, yo *k2, (k2tog, yo) 4 times; repeat from * to last st, k1.

Row 20: As Row 16.

Repeat rows 1–20 for Pattern B.

Pillow A

With A, cast on 83 stitches.

Work Pattern A until the Pillow measures 32" (81.5cm) from the cast-on edge, ending with RS facing for next row.

Bind off all stitches.

EDGING

With the circular needle, cast on 340 stitches.

Beginning with a purl row, work 3 rows in stockinette stitch.

Next row (RS): K4, *yo, k2tog, k2; repeat from * to end.

Work 3 rows stockinette stitch. Bind off all stitches.

FINISHING

Fold the Pillow in half and sew the sides together, leaving one side open to insert the pillow form. Insert the pillow form and sew opening closed with whipstitch (page 65). Sew the Edging around the pillow, easing it around the corners. Sew the Edging ends together.

Pillow B

With B, cast on 84 stitches.

Work Pattern B until the Pillow measures 32" (81.5cm) from the cast-on edge, ending with RS facing for next row.

Bind off all stitches.

FINISHING

Fold the Pillow in half and sew the sides together, leaving one side open to insert the pillow form. Insert the pillow form and sew the opening closed with whipstitch (page 65).

Ode to Jackie O

For a retro-feeling sweater, there is no better icon to ponder as a muse than the fashionable Jackie Onassis. Once I thought of Jackie, the collar on this sweater came in an instant.

Intermediate

SIZE

Small (Medium, Large, X-Large)

Bust: 30 (34½, 40, 45)" (76 [87, 101.5, 114.5]cm)

Finished size: 33 (38½, 43.75, 49)" (84 [98, 111, 124.5]cm)

MATERIALS

9 (9, 9, 10) hanks Classic Elite Yarns Montera (3 oz [100g]/127 yds [116m]; 50% llama/50% wool), #3825 Sunflower, (4) medium

1 pair US 9 (5.5mm) needles or size required to achieve gauge

1 cable needle

2 stitch holders

GAUGE

16 stitches and 21 rows = 4" (10cm) in stockinette stitch

21 stitches and 18 rows = 4" (10cm) in Cable and Lace Stitch.

STITCH PATTERN

CABLE AND LACE STITCH

Row 1 and All WS Rows (WS): K1, *p2tog, yo, p11, k1; repeat from * to end of row.
Row 2: K1, *ssk, yo, c6b, k6; repeat from * to end of row.
Row 4: K1, * ssk, yo, k12; repeat from * to end of row.
Row 6: K1, * ssk, yo, k3, c6f, k3; repeat from * to end of row.
Row 8: As for row 4.
Repeat rows 1–8 for Cable and Lace Stitch.

Note The instructions are written for the smallest size. When changes are necessary for larger sizes, those instructions are enclosed in parentheses.

Back

**Cast on 76 (88, 102, 114) stitches.

Row 1 (RS): *K1, p1; repeat from * to end of row.

Repeat row 1 for seed stitch for 1" (2.5cm), ending with WS facing for next row and increasing 9 (11, 11, 13) stitches on last row—85 (99, 113, 127) stitches.

Work in Cable and Lace Stitch until the Back measures 14 (14½, 15, 15½)" (35.5 [37, 38, 39.5]cm) from the cast-on edge, ending with RS facing for next row.

ARMHOLE SHAPING

Bind off 5 (7, 9, 11) stitches at the beginning of the next 2 rows—75 (85, 95, 105) stitches. Continuing in Cable and Lace Stitch, decrease 1 stitch at each end of the needle on the next 4 (8, 10, 11) alternate rows—67 (69, 75, 83) stitches.**

Continue even until the armhole measures 9½ (10, 10½, 11)" (24 [25.5, 26.5, 28]cm), ending with RS facing for next row.

SHOULDER SHAPING

Bind off 6 (6, 7, 8) stitches at the beginning of the next 2 rows, then 6 (6, 7, 9) stitches at the beginning of the following 2 rows. Leave the remaining 43 (45, 47, 49) stitches on a stitch holder for back neck.

Front

Work from ** to ** as for the Back.

Continue in Cable and Lace Stitch until the armhole measures 5½ (5½, 6, 6)" (14 [14, 15, 15]cm), ending with RS facing for next row.

NECK SHAPING (LEFT SIDE)

Next Row Work in pattern for 26 (27, 30, 33) stitches, turn. Place remaining stitches on spare needle.

Continuing in Cable and Lace Stitch, decrease 1 stitch at the neck edge 14 (15, 16, 16) rows—12 (12, 14, 17) stitches.

Continue in Cable and Lace Stitch until the armhole measures 9½ (10, 10½, 11)" (24 [25.5, 26.5, 28]cm), ending with RS facing for next row.

SHOULDER SHAPING (LEFT SIDE)

Bind off 6 (6, 7, 8) stitches at the beginning of the next 2 alternate rows. Work 1 row even in pattern. Bind off the remaining 6 (6, 7, 9) stitches.

NECK SHAPING (RIGHT SIDE)

With RS facing, slip 15 (15, 15, 17) stitches from the spare needle onto a stitch holder. Join yarn and work in pattern to end of row.

Continuing in Cable and Lace Stitch, decrease 1 stitch at the neck edge on the next 14 (16, 16, 16) rows—12 (12, 14, 17) stitches.

Continue in Cable and Lace Stitch until the armhole measures 9½ (10, 10½, 11)" (24 [25.5, 26.5, 28]cm), ending with WS facing for next row.

SHOULDER SHAPING (RIGHT SIDE)

Bind off 6 (6, 7, 8) stitches at the beginning of the next 2 alternate rows. Work 1 row even in pattern. Bind off remaining 6 (6, 7, 9) stitches.

Sleeves (Make 2)

Cast on 28 (30, 32, 34) stitches. Work in seed stitch as given for the Back for 1" (2.5cm), ending with RS facing for next row and increasing 6 stitches evenly across the last row—34 (36, 38, 40) stitches.

Continuing in stockinette stitch, increase 1 stitch at each end of the needle on the 3rd and every following 6th (6th, 6th, 4th) row to 56 (60, 64, 68) stitches. Continue even in stockinette stitch until the Sleeve measures 14¾ (15½, 16, 16½)" (37.5 [39.5, 40.5, 42]cm) from the cast-on edge, ending with RS facing for next row.

SHAPE CAP

Bind off 5 (7, 9, 11) stitches at the beginning of the next 2 rows—46 stitches. Decrease 1 stitch at each end of the needle on next and every other row 12 times to 20 stitches, then 1 stitch at each end of the needle every row to 16 stitches. Bind off 3 stitches on the next 2 alternate rows. Bind off remaining 10 stitches.

Finishing

Block the pieces to the measurements. Sew the right shoulder seam.

COLLAR

With RS facing, pick up and knit 18 stitches down the left Front neck edge, knit 15 (15, 15, 17) from the Front neck stitch holder, pick up and knit 18 stitches up the right Front neck edge, and 43 (47, 47, 49) from the Back neck stitch holder—94 (98, 98, 102) stitches.

Work in stockinette stitch until the collar measures 4" (10cm), ending with RS facing for next row. Bind off.

Sew the left shoulder seam. Sew the side and Sleeve seams. Fold the collar to the inside and sew into place, using whipstitch (pg 65).

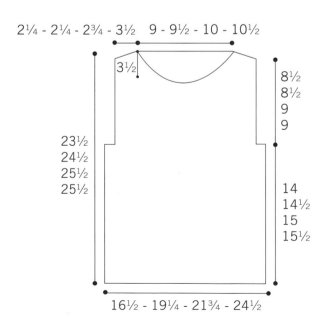

2¼ - 2¼ - 2¾ - 3½   9 - 9½ - 10 - 10½

3½

8½
8½
9
9

23½
24½
25½
25½

14
14½
15
15½

16½ - 19¼ - 21¾ - 24½

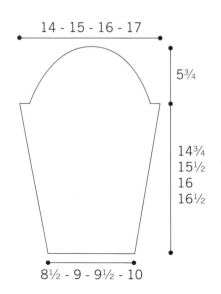

14 - 15 - 16 - 17

5¾

14¾
15½
16
16½

8½ - 9 - 9½ - 10

Summer Chill Shawl

Everyone needs a lacy summer shawl for chilly evenings or when at the computer working.
I love the "rhythm" of knitting this pattern.

Experienced

SIZE
50" (127cm) wide by 34"
(86.5cm) tall

MATERIALS
7 balls Classic Elite Yarns
Charmed (1¾ oz [50g]/130 yds
[119m]; 85% cashmere/15%
mohair) #76708 Heathered

Rose, (4) medium

1 32" (80cm) US 8 (5mm)
circular needle or size required
to obtain gauge

1 pair US 8 (5mm) needles

GAUGE
18 stitches and 21 rows =
4" (10cm) in stockinette stitch

Shawl

With circular needle, cast on 1 stitch.

Row 1 (RS) Kf&b&f.

Row 2 Purl.

Row 3 K1, yo, k1, yo, k1. 5 stitches

Row 4 Purl.

Work Chart A, reading all white spaces as stitches and ignoring the gray, to the end, reading all RS rows from right to left and WS rows from left to right.

Tip Mark each full repeat with a stitch marker to keep your place.

Work Chart B. Note that where a (sl1, k2tog, psso) cannot be made at an edge a (ssk, yo) for the right hand side or (yo, k2tog) for the left hand side will be worked. As soon you can, fit a full 6-stitch repeat in and continue to do so as stitches increase.

Continue until there are 345 stitches, ending with RS facing for next row and casting on 7 stitches at the end of the last row for the Edging

With straight needles, k6, k2tog (using 1 stitch from the shawl and 1 stitch from the Edging).

Knit 1 row. Proceed with Edging as follows:

Row 1 Sl1, k2, yfwd, k2tog, yfwd 2 times, k2tog.

Row 2 Yon, k2, p1 (into previous yfwd) k2, yfwd, k2tog, k2tog (with shawl edge st).

Row 3 Sl1, k2, yfwd, k2tog, k4.

Row 4 K6, yfwd, k2tog, k2tog (with shawl edge st).

Row 5 Sl1, k2, yfwd, (k2tog, yfwd 2 times) twice, k2tog.

Row 6 (K2, p1 [into previous yfwd]) 2 times, k2, yfwd, k2tog, k2tog (with shawl edge st).

Row 7 Sl1, k2, yfwd, k2tog, k6.

Row 8 K8, yfwd, k2tog, k2tog (with shawl edge st).

Row 9 Sl1, k2, yfwd, k2tog, (yfwd 2 times, k2tog) 3 times.

Row 10 (K2, p1 [into previous yfwd]) 3 times, k2, yfwd, k2tog, k2tog (with shawl edge st).

Row 11 Sl1, k2, yfwd, k2tog, k9.

Row 12 Bind off 7 stitches, yfwd, k2tog, k2tog (with shawl edge st).

Repeat rows 1–12 for Edging.

Continue working Edging to 2 stitches before center point, ending with Row 3. Work Row 4 of Edging, ending with k3tog (2 shawl stitches and 1 edging stitch to form a point).

Next Row K2tog (2 shawl stitches and 1 edging stitch). Work to end of shawl and knit 7. Then bind off these 7 stitches.

Reading Lace Charts

On the charts for the Summer Chill
Shawl, the center stitch is marked as blue
and remains vertically straight through the
middle of the shawl. Place a marker on
either side of the center stitch. The shaded
areas of the chart should be ignored; only
read the white areas. The right-side rows
are read right to left and the wrong-side
rows are read left to right. As you progress,
you will be repeating the six stitches
between the red lines.

Chart A

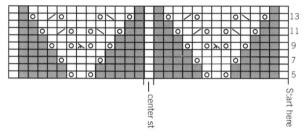

Chart B

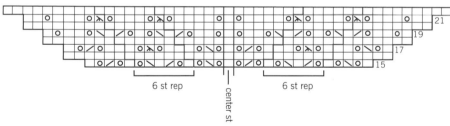

Chart C

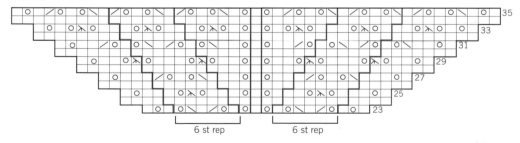

☐ = Knit on RS. Purl on WS.
◎ = Yarn over
⋏ = Sl1, K2tog, Psso
◢ = K2tog
◥ = Ssk

SEPTEMBER

AS BITTERSWEET AS IT IS to see the summer go, I love the colors and fashions the Fall brings. This is sweater season. As a magazine junkie, I get excited that this is the month that *Bazaar* and *Vogue* come out with issues so full of fall inspiration that they could double as dumbbells! Tweeds, silk scarves, and layers abound. Bounty is not just in the harvest—the fashion world is bursting at the seams. Knits are lavishly displayed in the windows at stores across the city. It doesn't get any better for the senses than fall.

I much prefer to knit with warm wools in September than with cool cottons in spring or summer. The smell and feel of merino wool does me in. Angora blends are begging to be rubbed on my cheek. A trip to any fiber festival is dangerous, brimming over with hundreds of balls and skeins; dripping with hanks of godly string; busting with knitting books and patterns. The Kitchener-Waterloo Knitter's Fair is a treat for knitters, some trailing suitcases on wheels, prepared for their purchases. If I were to head to a sale with a suitcase, my husband would hand me another filled with my clothes! But here lies the passion within all knitters, and September is the month to indulge in them!

We act as though comfort and luxury were the chief requirements of life, when all that we need to make us happy is something to be enthusiastic about.
—CHARLES KINGSLEY
(1819—1875)

Hip & Happenin' Wristwarmers

These are perfect for wearing as you type at the computer. Not only a great fashion look, they're practical, too, if you need dexterity in cold weather.

Beginner

SIZE
To fit an average-size woman's hand

MATERIALS
1 hank Manos del Uruguay Wool (3½ oz [100g/138 yds [126m]; 100% merino wool) #107 Purple/Plum, (**4**) medium

1 set of 4 US 8 (5mm) double-pointed needles

1 set of 4 US 9 (5.5mm) double-pointed needles or size required to achieve gauge

GAUGE
20 stitches and 26 rows = 4" (10cm) in stockinette stitch with larger needles

Left Hand

**With smaller needles, cast on 28 stitches. Divide the stitches onto three needles as follows: 12 stitches on needle 1, 8 stitches on needle 2, and 8 stitches on needle 3. Join to work in the round, and place marker.

Rnd 1 *K1, p1; repeat from * to end of round.

Repeat round 1 for (k1, p1) ribbing until the Left Hand measures 3" (7.75cm) from the cast-on edge.

Change to larger needles and knit 1 round.**

Proceed in Left Hand pattern stitch as follows:

Rnd 1 K2, yo, k3, sl1, k2tog, psso, k3, m1, k1, knit to end of round.

Rnd 2 and Alternate Rnds Knit.

Rnd 3 K3, m1, k2, sl1, k2tog, psso, k2, m1, k2, knit to end of round.

Rnd 5 K4, m1, k1, sl1, k2tog, psso, k1, m1, k3, knit to end of round.

Rnd 7 K5, m1, sl1, k2tog, psso, m1, k4, knit to end of round.

Rnd 8 Knit.

Tip On knit rnds, always knit an extra stitch from needle 2, onto needle 1 after every pattern round (so you will have enough stitches to do the k2tog on the next round).

THUMB OPENING

***Turn. Working back and forth across needle (not joining rnds), continue in pattern for 7 rows, noting that All WS Rows will be purled.

Join to work in the round and proceed as follows:

Next Rnd Knit.

Work 8 rnds in pattern.

Knit 2 rnds.

Bind off purlwise, and weave in the ends.***

Right Hand

Repeat from ** to ** as given for the Left Hand.

Proceed in Right Hand pattern stitch as follows:

Rnd 1 K16, yo, k3, sl1, k2tog, psso, k3, m1, k1.

Rnd 2 and Alternate Rnds Knit.

Rnd 3 K17, m1, k2, sl1, k2tog, psso, k2, m1, k2, knit to end of round.

Rnd 5 K18, m1, k1, sl1, k2tog, psso, k1, m1, k3, knit to end of round.

Rnd 7 K19, m1, sl1, k2tog, psso, m1, k4, knit to end of round.

Rnd 8 Knit.

Repeat from *** to *** as given for the Left Hand.

Tip In general, to prevent gaps in your work, whether working rows or rounds, pull the first few stitches (on each needle or each end of row) a little tighter than the rest.

College Daze

This one can be a belly flaunter with low-waisted jeans, but if you wish to cover up, just add rows before the armhole shaping. Don't panic, the dropped stitches are supposed to be there.

Intermediate

SIZE
Small (Medium, Large, X-Large)

Bust: 30 (34, 38, 42)" (76.25 [86.5, 96.5, 106.5]cm)

Finished size: 31 (35, 39, 42)" (78.5 [86.5, 99, 106.5]cm)

MATERIALS
8 (9, 9, 10) balls Needful Yarns Arte (1¾ oz [50g]/97 yds [90m]; 78% merino wool/ 19% acrylic/3% alpaca) #402, (4) medium

1 pair US 8 (5mm) needles or size required to achieve gauge

4 stitch holders.

GAUGE
15 stitches and 22 rows= 4" (10cm) in stockinette stitch

STITCH PATTERN
DROP-STITCH PATTERN

Row 1 (RS): P1 (1, 1, 0), *p7 (8, 9, 10), yo, p7 (8, 9, 10); repeat from * 3 times, p1 (1, 1, 0).

Rows 2–10: Knit.

Row 11: P1 (1, 1, 0), *p7 (8, 9, 10), drop the next stitch, letting it unravel down to the yo of row 1 (drop & open), p7 (8, 9, 10); repeat from * 3 times, p1 (1, 1, 0).

Rows 12–20: Work in reverse stockinette stitch.

Row 21: P1 (1, 1, 0), *p14 (16, 18, 20), yo; repeat from * 2 times, purl to end of row.

Rows 22–28: Work in reverse stockinette stitch.

Row 29: P1 (1, 1, 0), *p14 (16, 18, 20), drop & open next stitch; repeat from * 2 times, purl to end of row.

Repeat rows 1–29 rows for pattern.

Note The instructions are written for the smallest size. When changes are necessary for larger sizes, those instructions are enclosed in parentheses.

Back
Note Reverse stockinette stitch is RS for both Back and Front.

Cast on 58 (66, 74, 80) stitches.

Work in reverse stockinette stitch for 2" (5cm), ending with RS facing for next row.

Work Drop-Stitch Pattern once.

Continue in reverse stockinette stitch until work measures 10½ (11, 11½, 12)" (26.5 [28, 29, 30.5]cm) from the cast-on edge, ending with RS facing for next row.

RAGLAN SHAPING
Bind off 4 stitches at the beginning of the next 2 rows—50 (58, 66, 72) stitches.

Continuing in reverse stockinette stitch, decrease 1 stitch at each end of the needle on the next and every 6th (4th, 4th, 4th) row to 38 (38, 50, 60) stitches, then every 4th (2nd, 2nd, 2nd) row to 34 stitches.

Leave the remaining stitches on a stitch holder.

Front
Work as for the Back.

Sleeves (Make 2)
Note Stockinette stitch is RS for Sleeves.

Cast on 25 stitches.

Row 1 (RS) K1tbl, *p2, k1tbl; repeat from * to end.

Row 2 P1, *k1tbl, k1, p1; repeat from * to end.

Repeat rows 1–2 until the Sleeve measures 4" (10cm) from the cast-on edge, ending with RS facing for next row.

Next Row K1tbl, *sl next stitch off needle and allow to unravel to cast-on edge, p1, k1tbl; repeat from * to end—17 stitches.

Purl 1 row, increasing 9 stitches evenly across row—26 stitches.

Continuing in stockinette stitch, increase 1 stitch at each end of the needle on the next and every 12th (8th, 6th, 6th) row to 40 (42, 34, 44) stitches.

Sizes L and XL Only Increase 1 stitch at each end of the needle every 8th row to (44, 46) stitches.

All Sizes Continue even until the Sleeves measure 17" (43cm) from the cast-on edge, ending with RS facing for next row.

RAGLAN SHAPING

Bind off 4 stitches at the beginning of the next 2 rows—32 (34, 36, 38) stitches.

Continuing in stockinette stitch, decrease 1 stitch at each end of the needle on the next and every 4th row to 16 (18, 18, 20) stitches, then every 2nd row to 6 stitches.

Leave the remaining stitches on a stitch holder.

Finishing

Block the pieces to the measurements. Sew the armhole seams, leaving left Front raglan open.

COLLAR

With RS facing and smaller needles, pick up and knit 34 stitches from Front stitch holder, 6 stitches from right Sleeve stitch holder, 34 stitches from Back stitch holder, 6 stitches from left Sleeve stitch holder—80 stitches.

Work 2½" (6cm) in stockinette stitch, ending with RS facing for next row. Bind off all stitches. Sew the armhole seam to the beginning of the collar. Do not sew the collar; let it roll forward at the opening. Sew side and Sleeve seams.

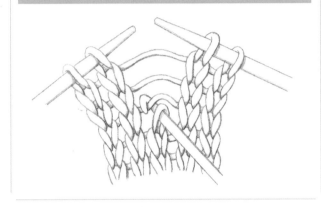

Dropping Stitches

I have purposely placed runs (that will stop) on the College Daze Sweater. But you may find you have dropped a stitch unknowingly, and you need to fix it. Crochet hooks are handy to have around for this purpose. Locate the bottom of the run, and place your hook into the stitch from front to back on the right side. Find the first horizontal strand above the dropped stitch and hook it from beneath. Pull this strand through the dropped stitch. Repeat for each strand until you reach the needles, and pop the stitch back onto the left needle, ready to work.

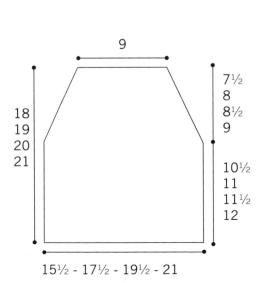

9

18
19
20
21

7½
8
8½
9

10½
11
11½
12

15½ - 17½ - 19½ - 21

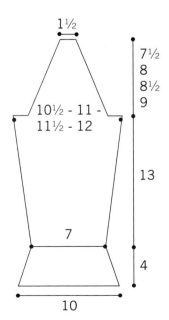

1½

7½
8
8½
9

10½ - 11 -
11½ - 12

13

7

4

10

What's His Is Hers Fair Isle V-Neck Vest

The look of menswear is great on women and the autumn season makes it easy to combine leather, grey flannel, and a classic fair isle vest with tie.

Experienced

SIZE
Small (Medium, Large, X-Large)

Bust: 30–32 (34–36, 38–40, 42–44)" (76–81 [86–91, 97–102, 107–112]cm)

Finished size: 34 (38, 43, 47)" (86.5 [96.5, 109, 119.5]cm)

MATERIALS
Blue Sky Alpacas Sport Weight (1¾ oz [50g]/110 yds [100m]; 100% alpaca), **2** fine
  2 (2, 3) hanks #512 Aubergine (MC)

2 hanks #05 Beige (A)
2 hanks #519 Gold (B)
2 hanks #10 Grey (C)
2 hanks #25 Olive (D)

1 pair US 4 (3.5mm) needles

1 pair US 6 (4mm) needles or size required to achieve gauge

1 stitch holder

1 safety pin

GAUGE
27 stitches and 28 rows = 4" (10cm) in Fair Isle pattern with larger needles

Note The instructions are written for the smallest size. When changes are necessary for larger sizes, those instructions are enclosed in parentheses.

Back

**With smaller needles and MC, cast on 102 (114, 134, 142) stitches.

Row 1 K2, *p2, k2; repeat from * to end of row.

Row 2 P2, *k2, p2; repeat from * to end of row.

Repeat rows 1–2 for ribbing until the Back measures 4" (10cm) from the cast-on edge, ending with RS facing for next row and increasing 13 (15, 11, 17) stitches on last row—115 (129, 145, 159) stitches.

Work Chart in stockinette stitch, reading knit rows from right to left and purl rows from left to right, ending with RS facing for next row. Continue working Chart until the Back measures 10¾ (10¾, 11¼, 11¼)" (27.5 [27.5, 28.5, 28.5]cm) from the beginning, ending with RS facing for next row. **

ARMHOLE SHAPING

Bind off 8 (9, 13, 14) stitches at the beginning of the next 2 rows. Continuing working Chart, decrease 1 stitch at each end of the needle on the next 9 (10, 13, 15) rows—81 (91, 93, 101) stitches.

Continue working Chart until the Back measures 18½ (19, 19½, 20)" (47 [48, 49.5, 51]cm) from the beginning, ending with RS facing for next row.

SHOULDER SHAPING

Bind off 6 (7, 8, 9) stitches at the beginning of the next 4 rows and then bind off 6 (8, 7, 8) stitches at the beginning of the next 2 rows. Leave the remaining 45 (47, 47, 49) stitches on a stitch holder for the Back neck.

Front

Work from ** to ** as for the Back.

ARMHOLE AND NECK SHAPING

Next Row Bind off 8 (9, 13, 14) stitches, k49 (55, 59, 65), including bind off stitch, turn. Leave the remaining stitches on spare needle.

Next Row K2tog, work to end of row from Chart.

Continue working Chart, decreasing 1 stitch at the armhole every row 8 (9, 12, 14) times, AT THE SAME TIME decrease 1 stitch at the neck edge every row to 18 (22, 23, 26) stitches. Continue in Chart as established until the Front measures 18½ (19, 19½, 20)" (47 [48.5, 49.5, 51]cm) from the cast-on edge, ending with RS facing for next row.

SHOULDER SHAPING

Bind off 6 (7, 8, 9) stitches at the beginning of the next 2 RS rows. Work 1 row even in pattern. Bind off remaining stitches.

Slip next stitch from the spare needle onto the safety pin (center stitch). Join another ball to the remaining stitches on the spare needle and work Chart to end of row.

Next row (WS) Bind off 8 (9, 13, 14) stitches.

Next Row Work 1 row even from Chart.

Next Row P2tog, then work even from Chart.

Continue Chart, decreasing 1 stitch at the armhole every row 8 (9, 12, 14) times, AT THE SAME TIME decrease 1 stitch at the neck edge every row to 18 (22, 23, 26) stitches. Continue in Chart as established until the Front measures 18½ (19, 19½, 20)" (47 [48, 49.5, 51]cm) from the cast-on edge, ending with WS facing for next row.

SHOULDER SHAPING

Bind off 6 (7, 8, 9) stitches at the beginning of the next and the next 2 WS rows. Work 1 row even in pattern. Bind off remaining stitches.

Finishing

Block the pieces to the measurements. Sew the right and left shoulder seams.

NECKBAND

With RS facing, MC, and smaller needles, pick up and knit 38 (38, 40, 40) stitches down the left Front neck.
Knit the stitch from the safety pin (center stitch) and place a marker by it. Pick up and knit 38 (38, 40, 40) stitches up the right Front neck. Knit across 45 (47, 47, 49) stitches from the Back neck stitch holder—122 (124, 128, 130) stitches.

Row 1 Work in ribbing as given for the Back to center 5 stitches, p2tog, p1, p2togtbl, work in ribbing to end.

Row 2 (WS) Work in ribbing to center 5 stitches, k2tog, k1, sl1, k1, psso, work in ribbing to end of row.

Repeat rows 1–2 for 1" (2.5cm), ending with RS facing for next row.

Bind off all stitches in ribbing, decreasing 1 stitch at center front by working 2 stitches together before binding off.

ARMBANDS

With RS facing, MC, and smaller needles, pick up and knit 78 (78, 82, 82) stitches around the armhole. Work in ribbing as given for the Back for 1" (2.5cm). Bind off in ribbing.

Sew the side seams.

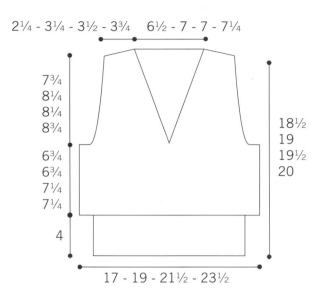

2¼ - 3¼ - 3½ - 3¾   6½ - 7 - 7 - 7¼

7¾
8¼
8¼
8¾

6¾
6¾
7¼
7¼

4

18½
19
19½
20

17 - 19 - 21½ - 23½

Stranding in Fair Isle

If you strand unused yarn for more than 3 stitches, you run the risk if getting rings or fingers caught when you go to put on the garment. Also, by limiting the stranding to every 2 to 3 stitches, you will have a neater looking wrong side. I always see proud Fair Isle knitters show off the wrong side of their work! Also, be mindful of your tension. Too tight or too loose will spoil the look of your work.

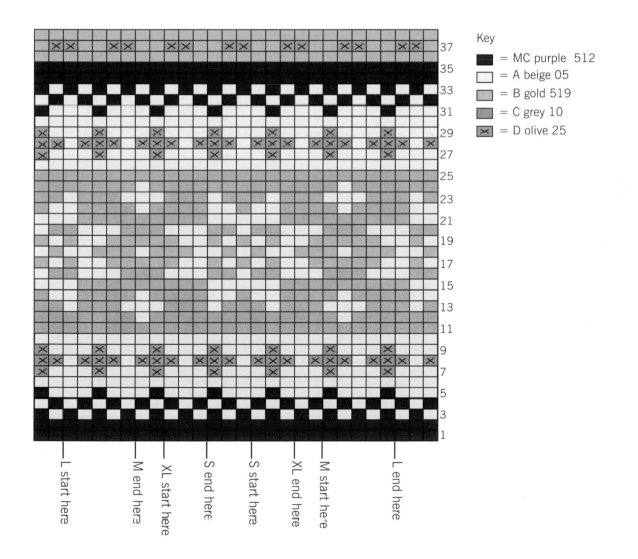

Key

■ = MC purple 512

□ = A beige 05

■ = B gold 519

■ = C grey 10

⊠ = D olive 25

L start here

M end here

XL start here

S end here

S start here

XL end here

M start here

L end here

OCTOBER

A LOT OF KNITTING IS DONE this month to prepare for gifts for the holiday season or to simply create the cozy knits we'll need to keep warm for the winter season! My daughters will pick up the needles and share with me their ideas and designs. Knitting is the gift so many mothers have passed onto their daughters, and it is a gift we mothers hope they will share with their own children. Knitting is one of the traditions that continues to be relevant in our increasingly busy lives because it calms us and brings us together. It is a craft that continues to link families and friends, as we share our knitting stories, yarns, patterns, and gifts.

No act of kindness, no matter how small, is ever wasted.

—AESOP (620 BC–560 BC), THE LION AND THE MOUSE

125

128

131

Kimono Wrap

This feels cozy, like a blanket with sleeves should. This simple construction yields big results.

Beginner

SIZE
Small (Medium, Large)

Bust: 30 (34, 36)" (76 [86.5, 91.5]cm)

Finished size: 17 (18, 19)" (43 [45.5, 48]cm) across back

MATERIALS
8 skeins Manos del Uruguay Wool (3½ oz [100g/138 yds [126m]; 100% merino wool) #03 Lavender, **(4)** medium

1 36" (90cm) US 8 (5mm) circular needle or size required to achieve gauge

Note Because of the distinctive tones of each skein, it is recommended that you work 2 rows from one skein and then 2 rows from another skein to even out the dyes.

2 spare needles

GAUGE
16 stitches and 24 rows= 4" (10cm) in Pattern Stitch

STITCH PATTERN
PATTERN STITCH
Row 1 (RS): (K1, p1) twice, *k4, (k1, p1) twice; repeat from * to end of row.
Row 2: (P1, k1) twice, *p4, (p1, k1) twice; repeat from * to end of row.
Repeat rows 1–2 for Pattern Stitch.

Note The instructions are written for the smallest size. When changes are necessary for larger sizes, those instructions are enclosed in parentheses.

Body

**Cast on 188 (196, 212) stitches.

Work in Pattern Stitch for 12½ (13½, 14½)" (32 [34.5, 37]cm), ending with RS facing for next row.

DIVIDE FOR ARMHOLES

Next Row Work in pattern across 60 (62, 68) stitches, turn. Leave the remaining stitches on a spare needle.

Next Row Continue in pattern on these 60 (62, 68) stitches for Left Front until the armhole measures 8 (9, 10)" (20.5 [23, 25.5]cm), ending with WS facing for next row. Slip these stitches on a long length of yarn.

With RS of work facing, join yarn to the remaining stitches on the spare needle, and work in pattern across 68 (72, 76) stitches for the Back, turn.

Leave the remaining stitches on the spare needle.

Continue in pattern until the armhole measures 8 (9, 10)" (20.5 [23, 25.5]cm), ending with WS facing for next row. Slip these stitches on a long length of yarn.

With RS of work facing, join yarn to the remaining stitches on the spare needle and work in pattern to end of row for the right front—60 (62, 68) stitches.

Continue in pattern until the armhole measures 8 (9, 10)" (20.5 [23, 25.5]cm), ending with WS facing for next row.

JOINING ROW

Work in pattern across 60 (62, 68) stitches of the right front, 68 (72, 76) stitches from length of yarn for the back, and 60 (62, 68) stitches from length of yarn for the left front. 188 (196, 212) stitches.

Continue in pattern until the work measures 25½ (27½, 29½)" (65 [70, 75]cm) from the cast-on edge, ending with WS facing for next row.

Dyes

Unless you have a knowledgeable salesperson helping you when buying yarn, you may not know about dye lots. Aside from a color name and number, the ball band will also tell you a dye lot number. Buying more than one ball means you have to make sure the dye lot numbers are the same, or you may end up with a sleeve that is a different shade than the body. Manos yarn, used here in the Kimono Wrap, doesn't have dye lots, and because of the variegation of color, it is wise to change skeins every 2 rows over a large body of knitting to minimize the differences between skeins.

FOLD-BACK COLLAR

Row 1 (RS) (K1, p1) twice, *k4, k1, p1; repeat from * to end of row.

Row 2 (P1, k1) twice, *p4, p1, k1; repeat from * to end of row.

Repeat rows 1–2 for 6½ (7, 7½)" (16.5 [18, 19]cm), ending with RS facing for next row. Bind off all stitches.

Sleeves (make 2)

Cast on 44 stitches.

Work in Pattern Stitch as given for the Body, increasing 1 stitch at each end of the needle on the 3rd and every following 8th (6th, 4th) rows 1 (5, 2) times to 46 (54, 48) stitches, then every following 10th (8th, 6th) row to 64 (72, 80) stitches, taking increased stitches into pattern.

Continue in pattern until the Sleeve measure 19" (48.5cm), ending with RS facing for next row. Bind off all stitches.

Finishing

Block the pieces to the measurements. Sew in the sleeves.

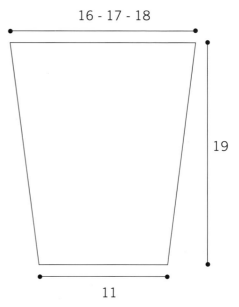

16 - 17 - 18

19

11

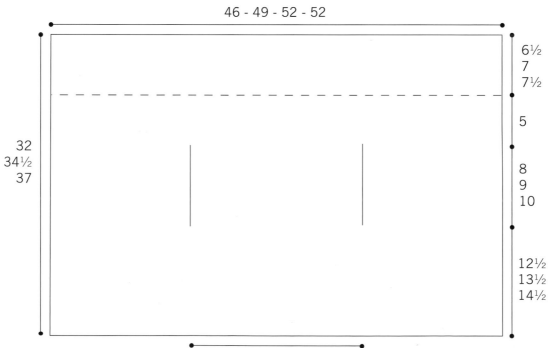

46 - 49 - 52 - 52

6½
7
7½

5

8
9
10

12½
13½
14½

32
34½
37

17 - 18 - 19

Doggy Doodle

It is no secret to those who know me that Patons Classic Merino is one of my favorite basic wools. It is soft, comfortable to wear, and easy to knit with. There was a time when I was designing dog coat after dog coat—it was as amusing as designing for kids! You can pump up the color and the fun.

Intermediate

SIZE
Small (Medium, Large)

Chest: 14 (16, 24)" (35.5 [40.5, 61]cm)

MATERIALS
Patons Classic Merino Wool (3½ oz [100g]/223 yds [200m]; 100% merino wool), **(3)** light

1 ball #212 Royal Purple (MC)
1 ball #218 Peacock (A)
1 ball #240 Leaf Green (B)
1 ball #202 Aran (C)
1 ball #238 Paprika (D)
1 ball #226 Black (E)

1 36" (90cm) US 6 (4mm) circular needle

1 36" (90cm) US 7 (4.5mm) circular needle or size required to obtain gauge

1 set US 6 (4mm) double-pointed needles

1 stitch holder

GAUGE
20 stitches and 26 rows = 4" (10cm) in stockinette stitch with larger needles

21 stitches and 25 rows = 4" (10cm) in Fair Isle pattern with larger needles

Note The instructions are written for the smallest size. When changes are necessary for larger sizes, those instructions are enclosed in parentheses.

Body

With smaller circular needle and MC, cast on 54 (82, 110) stitches. Working back and forth, proceed as follows:

Row 1 K2, *p2, k2; repeat from * to end.

Row 2 P2, *k2, p2; repeat from * to end.

Repeat rows 1–2 for ribbing to 1½ (1½, 2)" (4 [4, 5]cm), increasing 2 stitches evenly across the last row, ending with RS facing for next row. 56 (66, 92) stitches.

Change to larger needles and work Chart in stockinette stitch to end of chart, noting 28 stitch repeat will be worked 1 (2, 3) time(s), reading RS rows from right to left and WS rows from left to right, AT THE SAME TIME, increase 1 stitch at each end of the needle on next 9 (11, 7) rows, working extra stitches in Chart—74 (106, 126) stitches.

Work even in pattern, repeating 28-stitch repeat of Chart until the work measures 4¼ (5, 8½)" (11 [12.5, 21.5]cm) from the cast-on edge, ending with RS facing for next row.

LEG OPENING

Next Row Continuing in Chart, work 6 (12, 13) stitches, bind off next 7 (8, 12) stitches, work in pattern to last 13 (20, 25) stitches, bind off next 7 (8, 12) stitches, work in pattern to end of row.

Using separate ball of yarn for each leg section, continue in chart for 1½ (2, 2½)" (4 [5, 6]cm) from bind-off row, ending with RS facing for next row.

JOINING

Work in pattern for 6 (12, 13) stitches, turn. Cast on 7 (8, 12) stitches, turn. Work in pattern to end of row, casting on 7 (8, 12) stitches over bind-off stitches—74 (106, 126) stitches.

Work in pattern until the work measures 7 (8½, 12)" (18 [21.5, 30.5]cm) from the cast-on edge, ending with RS facing for next row. PM (place marker).

CHEST SHAPING

Continuing in Chart, bind off 3 stitches at the beginning of the next 2 rows—68 (100, 120) stitches.

Decrease Row (RS) K1, sl1, psso, work in pattern to last 3 stitches, k2tog, k1.

Next Row Work in pattern to end of row.

Repeat the last 2 rows until 42 (48, 74) stitches remain.

Work even in pattern until work measures 12½ (15½, 21)" (32 [39.5, 53.5]cm) from the cast-on edge or to desired length to base of tail. Place stitches on the stitch holder.

Finishing

Join chest seam.

BODY RIBBING

With RS facing, MC, and smaller needle, pick up and knit 51
(60, 77) stitches from chest seam to stitch holder, knit 42
(48, 74) stitches from the stitch holder, pick up and knit 51
(60, 77) stitches to chest seam. 144 (168, 228) stitches.
Join to work in the round, placing marker at the beginning of
the round. Work in (k2, p2) ribbing for 1" (2.5cm). Bind off in
ribbing.

LEG RIBBING

With RS facing and double-pointed needle, pick up and knit
28 (32, 48) stitches around leg opening. Divide stitches onto
3 needles. Work in (k2, p2) ribbing for 1" (2.5cm). Bind off.

Knitting for Dogs

**When knitting for dogs, it is important
to take their measurements accurately.
Their chest is measured from behind
their front legs, sometimes refered to as
girth. The length is measured from the
base of its neck (where the collar lies) to
the base of its tail.**

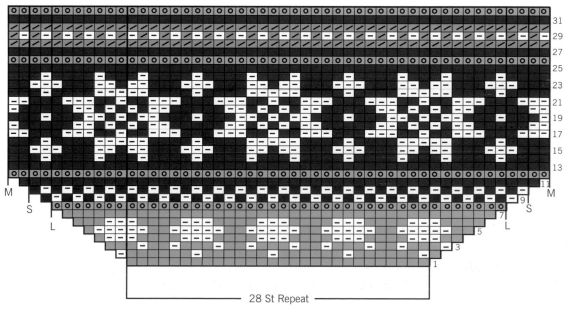

Key

■	= MC
■	= A
⊙	= B
⊟	= C
⟋	= D
■	= E

28 St Repeat

Out in the Woods Sweater

This is a quintessential all-over cable that will keep you happily challenged, yet you will eventually memorize the cable pattern. I have experimented with different yarns for this pattern and all work great with it. I especially like the look tweedy yarns give here.

Experienced

SIZE
Small (Medium, Large, X-Large, XX-Large)

Bust: 30–32 (34–36, 38–40, 42–44, 46–8)" (76–81.5 [86.5–91.5, 96.5–101.5, 106.5–112, 117–122]cm)

Finished size: 38 (42½, 47½, 52, 57)" (96.5 [108, 120.5, 132, 144.5]cm)

MATERIALS
19 (19, 20, 21, 23) balls Classic Elite Yarns Skye Tweed (1¾ oz [50g/110 yds [100m]; 100% wool) #1257 Blue River (his) or #1232 Paisley Pink (hers), (4) medium

8 (9, 9, 9, 9) hanks Briggs & Little Regal 2 ply (4 oz [113g]/272 yds [250m];

100% pure new wool) Lilac, (4) medium

1 pair US 7 (4.5mm) needles or size required to obtain gauge

1 stitch holder

1 cable needle

GAUGE
20 stitches and 26 rows = 4" (10cm) in stockinette stitch

STITCH PATTERN
EXCHANGE CABLE PATTERN

Row 1 (RS): P2, k4, *p4, k4; repeat from * to last 2 stitches, p2.
Row 2: K2, p4, *k4, p4; repeat from * to last 2 stitches, k2.
Row 3: P2, c4f, p4, c4b, *p4, c4f, p4, c4b; repeat from * to last 2 stitches, p2.
Row 4: As for row 2.
Rows 5–8: Repeat rows 1–4.

Row 9: P1, t3b, t4f, t4b, t3f, *p2, t3b, t4f, t4b, t3f; repeat from * to last stitch, p1.
Row 10: K1, p2, k3, p4, k3, p2, *k2, p2, k3, p4, k3, p2; repeat from * to last stitch, k1.
Row 11: P1, k2, p3, c4b, p3, k2, *p2, k2, p3, c4b, p3, k2; repeat from * to last stitch, p1.
Row 12: As for row 10.
Row 13: P1, t3f, t4b, t4f, t3b, *p2, t3f, t4b, t4f, t3b; repeat from * to last stitch, p1.
Row 14: As for row 2.
Row 15: P2, c4b, p4, c4f, *p4, c4b, p4, c4f; repeat from * to last 2 stitches, p2.
Row 16: As for row 2.
Row 17: As for row 1.
Rows 18–21: Repeat rows 14–17.
Rows 22–24: Repeat rows 14–16.

Row 25: P1, t3b, t3f, p2, t3b, *t4f, t4b, t3f, p2, t3b; repeat from * to last 4 stitches, t3f, p1.
Row 26: K1, p2, (k2, p2) twice, *k3, p4, k3, p2, k2, p2; repeat from * to last 5 stitches, k2, p2, k1.
Row 27: P1, k2, (p2, k2) twice, *p3, c4f, p3, k2, p2, k2; repeat from * to last 5 stitches, p2, k2, p1.
Row 28: As for row 26.
Row 29: P1, t3f, t3b, p2, t3f, *t4b, t4f, t3b, p2, t3f; repeat from * to last 4 stitches, t3b, p1.
Rows 30–32: Repeat rows 2–4.

Repeat rows 1–32 for Exchange Cable Pattern.

Note The instructions are written for the smallest size. When changes are necessary for larger sizes, those instructions are enclosed in parentheses.

Back

**Cast on 128 (144, 160, 176, 192) stitches.

Work in Exchange Cable Pattern until the Back measures 16½ (16½, 16½, 17, 17)" (42 [42, 42, 43, 43]cm) from the cast-on edge, ending with RS facing for next row.

ARMHOLE SHAPING

Bind off 6 (9, 9, 11, 10) stitches at the beginning of the next 2 rows—116 (126, 142, 154, 172) stitches.**

Continue in Exchange Cable Pattern until the back measures 25½ (26, 26½, 27, 27½)" (65 [66, 67.5, 68.5, 70]cm) from the cast-on edge, ending with RS facing for next row.

SHOULDER SHAPING

Bind off 11 (13, 15, 17, 19) stitches at the beginning of the next 4 rows, then 12 (12, 14, 16, 20) stitches at the beginning of the next 2 rows. Leave the remaining 48 (50, 54, 54, 56) stitches on a stitch holder.

Front

Work from ** to ** as given for the Back.

Continue in pattern until the Front measures 22½ (23, 23½, 24, 24½)" (57 [58.5, 59.5, 61, 62]cm) from the cast-on edge, ending with RS facing for next row.

NECK SHAPING (LEFT SIDE)

Next Row Work in pattern for 45 (50, 57, 63, 71) stitches (neck edge), turn. Leave the remaining stitches on a spare needle.

Decrease 1 stitch (work 2 stitches together) at the neck edge on the next 9 (10, 11, 11, 11) rows, then every 2nd row twice—34 (38, 44, 50, 58) stitches.

6 - 6¾ - 7¾ - 9 - 10   7 - 7½ - 8 - 8 - 8¼

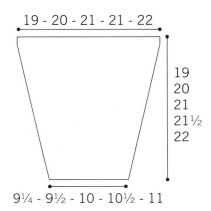

26
26½
27
27½
28

9.5
10
10½
10½
11

16½
16½
16½
17
17

19 - 21¼ - 23¾ - 26 - 28½

19 - 20 - 21 - 21 - 22

19
20
21
21½
22

9¼ - 9½ - 10 - 10½ - 11

Continue even in pattern until the Front measures 25½ (26, 26½, 27, 27½)" (65 [66, 67.5, 68.5, 70]cm) from the cast-on edge, ending with RS facing for next row.

SHOULDER SHAPING (LEFT SIDE)

Bind off 11 (13, 15, 17, 19) stitches at the beginning of the next 2 RS rows. Work 1 row even. Bind off remaining 12 (12, 14, 16, 20) stitches.

NECK SHAPING (RIGHT SIDE)

Slip the next 26 (26, 28, 28, 30) stitches from the spare needle onto a stitch holder. Work in pattern to end of row on remaining stitches. Decrease 1 stitch (work 2 stitches together) at the neck edge on the next 9 (10, 11, 11, 11) rows, then every 2nd row twice—34 (38, 44, 50, 58) stitches.

Continue even in pattern until the Front measures 25½ (26, 26½, 27, 27½)" (65 [66, 67.5, 68.5, 70]cm) from the cast-on edge, ending with WS facing for next row.

SHOULDER SHAPING (RIGHT SIDE)

Bind off 11 (13, 15, 17, 19) stitches at the beginning of the next 2 WS rows. Work 1 row even. Bind off remaining 12 (12, 14, 16, 20) stitches.

Sleeves (Make 2)

Cast on 64 (64, 64, 72, 72) stitches.

Sizes S, M, and L Only

Row 1 (RS) P2, k4, *p4, k4; repeat from * to last 2 stitches, p2.

Row 2 K2, p4, *k4, p4; repeat from * to last 2 stitches, k2.

Row 3 P1, M1P, p1, c4f, p4, c4b, *p4, c4f, p4, c4b; repeat from * to last 2 stitches, p1, M1P, p1.

Row 4 K3, p4, *k4, p4; repeat from * to last 3 stitches, k3.

Sleeve is now ready for the Exchange Cable Pattern.

Sizes XL and XXL Only

Row 1 (RS) K2, *p4, k4; repeat from * to last 6 stitches, p4, k2.

Row 2 P2, *k4, p4; repeat from * to last 6 stitches, k4, p2.

Row 3 K1, M1L, k1, *p4, c4f, p4, c4b; repeat from * to last 6 stitches, p4, k1, M1R, k1.

Row 4 P3, *k4, p4; repeat from * to last 6 stitches, k4, p3.

Sleeve is now ready for the Exchange Cable Pattern.

All Sizes

Continuing in Exchange Cable Pattern, increase 1 stitch at each end of the needle on the next and every 2nd row to 70 (80, 92, 88, 92) stitches, then every following 4th row to 122 (128, 136, 136, 142) stitches, taking increased stitches into the pattern.

Continue in pattern until the Sleeve measures 19 (19, 20, 20, 21)" (48 [48, 51, 51, 53.5]cm) from the cast-on edge, ending with RS facing for next row.

Place markers at each end of the last row.

Work 8 (10, 10, 12, 12) rows even. Bind off all stitches.

Finishing

Pin all pieces to measurements and cover with a damp cloth. Leave the cloth to dry on the garment.

NECKBAND

Sew the right shoulder seam. With RS of work facing, pick up and knit 26 stitches down the left Front neck edge. Knit across 26 (26, 28, 28, 30) stitches from front stitch holder, decreasing 1 stitch at center, by working 2 stitches together. Pick up and knit 26 stitches up the right Front neck edge. Knit across 48 (50, 54, 54, 56) stitches from the Back stitch holder, decreasing 3 stitches, by working 2 stitches together, evenly across—122 (122, 130, 130, 134) stitches.

Next row (WS) P2, *k2, p2; repeat from * to end of row.

Next Row K2, *p2, k2; repeat from * to end of row.

Repeat the last two rows for ribbing for 4" (10cm), ending with WS facing for next row.

Bind off loosely in ribbing. Sew the left shoulder and neckband seams. Fold the neckband in half to the wrong side and sew in position.

Sew the sleeves and side seams.

Customizing Your Knits

Don't be afraid to personalize your sweaters. You can make the borders deeper, the length of the body or sleeves longer, and the body wider. The trick to changing the length is to do it before you reach the armholes. The sleeve is a piece of the puzzle that is made to fit into the armhole perfectly, so we don't want to change anything from the armhole up.
If you change the length before the armhole, you can add length to the sleeves between the increases.

NOVEMBER

IMAGINE HAVING ALL YOUR GIFTS ready in November and having more time to decorate the house, bake, socialize and, of course, knit. This month, projects are small and make great stocking stuffers or gifts for hostesses. There is something nice about spending a Saturday afternoon knitting by the fire, when you know there is a parking kerfuffle going on somewhere at the super center. Who needs the stress?

Everybody loves receiving handmade hats and mitts as gifts, and ones knit in Manos yarn will be sure to please. And knitting up stash-busting scarves for yourself (Scarf #2 is my favorite) or loved ones makes a gift for you both. The Turtle Doves (page 139) make lovely ornaments that can double as bottle adornments. They are also a fun and easy project to get the kids involved with. Above all, you can breeze into December relaxed and ready for the fun and excitement!

Happiness does not notice the passing of time.
—CHINESE PROVERB.

137

139

140

49th Parallel Hat and Mitts

I live south of the 49th parallel in Canada, but these warm knits are still necessities! Everyone needs a basic, quick-knitting hat and mitten pattern, and this is it. You can knit a second pair in the next size up, felt it slightly, and use as an insert for extra warmth.

Intermediate

SIZE

MITTS

Small (Medium, Large)

7½ (8½, 11½)" (19 [21.5, 29]cm)

HAT

To fit a 21½" (54.5cm) circumference head

MATERIALS

Manos del Uruguay Wool (3½ oz [100]g/138yd [126m]; 100% wool), (4) medium

Hers: MC: (Mitts #100 Agate Multi) 1 hank, His: MC: (Mitts #55 Olive) 1 hank, (Hat # 101 Jungle Multi) 1 hank.

NOTE 1 hank will make a hat and mitts.

MITTS

1 set of four US 9 (5.5mm) double-pointed needles or size required to achieve gauge

HAT

1 pair US 9 (5.5mm) needles or size required to achieve gauge

GAUGE

18 stitches and 30 rows = 4" (10cm) in stockinette stitch

Note The instructions are written for the smallest size. When changes are necessary for larger sizes, those instructions are enclosed in parentheses.

Mitts (Make 2)

Cast on 20 (28, 36) stitches. Divide stitches evenly on 3 needles. Join to work in the round and place marker (PM).

Rnd 1 *K2, p2. Repeat from * to end of round.

Repeat round 1 for 2 (2½, 3)" (5 [6, 7.5]cm), increasing 2 (2, 0) stitches evenly across last round—22 (30, 36) stitches.

Next Rnd Knit, increasing 1 stitch at the end of the round—23 (31, 37) stitches.

THUMB GUSSET

Next Rnd K23 (31, 37) stitches, PM, M1L, k1, M1R, PM, knit to end—25 (33, 39) stitches.

Next Rnd Knit.

Next Rnd Slip marker, M1L, knit to next marker, M1R, slip marker, knit to end.

Continue in this manner, increasing 2 stitches every 2nd row until there are 31 (41, 49) stitches, 11 (13, 15) thumb gusset stitches. Place thumb stitches on a spare piece of yarn. Cast on 1 stitch and knit to end of round—23 (31, 37) stitches.

HAND

Work even in stockinette stitch in the round until the Mitt measures 5½ (7½, 9½)" (14 [19, 24]cm) from the cast-on edge or to 1 (1½, 2)" (2.5 [4, 5]cm) less than the desired length.

Next Rnd Decrease 3 (3, 1) stitches evenly around—20 (28, 36) stitches.

MITT TOP

Rnd 1 Sl1, k1, psso, k6 (10, 14), k2tog, sl1, k1, psso, k6 (10, 14), k2tog—16 (24, 32) stitches.

Rnd 2 Knit.

Rnd 3 Knit.

Repeat rounds 1–3 until there are 16 stitches remaining, then repeat row 1 only until there are 8 stitches remaining.
Break the yarn, leaving a long end. Graft the stitches together. (See page 138.)

Row 7 *K1, p1, k2tog, p1; repeat from * to end of row—44 stitches.

Row 9 *K2tog, k1, p1; repeat from * to end of row—33 stitches.

Row 11 *K2tog, p1; repeat from * to end of row—22 stitches.

Row 13 *K2tog; repeat from * to end of row—11 stitches.

Next Row K1, *k2tog; repeat from * to end of row—6 stitches.

Break yarn, leaving a long end. Draw the yarn through the remaining stitches and pull tight. Sew the center back seam.

THUMB

Divide thumb stitches onto 3 needles. Pick up and knit 1 stitch over the gap. Join to work in the round—12 (14, 16) stitches. Work even in stockinette stitch for 1 (1½, 2)" (2.5 [4, 5]cm).

Next Row *K2tog; repeat from * to end of round—6 (7, 8) stitches.

Next Row Knit.

Next Row K0 (1, 0), *k2tog; repeat from * to end of round. 3 (4, 4) stitches.

Break the yarn, leaving a long end. Draw the yarn through the remaining stitches and pull tight. Weave in the end.

Hat

Cast on 88 stitches.

Row 1 (RS) *K2, p2; repeat from * to end of row.

Repeat this row for ribbing until the Hat measures 6½" (16.5cm) from the cast-on edge.

HAT TOP

Row 1 (RS) *K2, p2, k2, p2tog; repeat from * to end of row—77 stitches.

Row 2 and All WS Rows Knit the knit stitches and purl the purl stitches.

Row 3 *K2, p2tog, k2, p1; repeat from * to end of row—66 stitches.

Row 5 *K2tog, p1, k2, p1; repeat from * to end of row—55 stitches.

Kitchener Stitch (Grafting)

Grafting is one of those techniques that must be started properly, or the rest is a mess. With your tapestry needle threaded and needles held together with the wrong sides facing each other, insert the tapestry needle into the first stitch on the front needle as if to purl. *Insert the needle knitwise into the first stitch on the back needle. Then insert the needle knitwise into the same first stitch on the front needle, and let the stitch fall off the needle. Pull gently to tighten. Insert the needle into next stitch on the front needle purlwise, then insert it into the first stitch on the back needle purlwise, and slip that stitch off the needle. Then insert the needle knitwise into the new first stitch on the back needle. Repeat from * until all the stitches have been grafted together. In your head, you can chant "Front knitwise off, front purlwise, back purlwise off, back knitwise" to remember your steps.

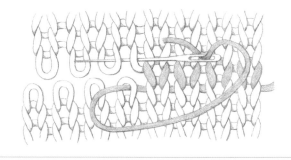

Turtle Doves

*With the variety in Christmas trees available now, I wanted to make ornaments that would look
magical on a white tree. But you can use colors that coordinate with your tree and decorations.
This pattern makes nine Turtle Dove ornaments.*

Beginner

SIZE
Appoximately 3" x 5" (7.5cm x
12.5cm) finished

MATERIALS
Patons Classic Merino Wool
(3½ oz [100g]/223 yds
[204m]; 100% merino wool),
(4) medium

2 balls each #210 Petal,

#77117 Worn Denim,
#203 Maize

1 pair US 7 (4.5mm) needles or
size required to achieve gauge

1 tapestry needle

Polyester toy stuffing

GAUGE
20 stitches and 26 rows= 4"
(10cm) in stockinette stitch

Panels (Make 6 in Each Color)

Cast on 40 stitches.

Work in stockinette stitch for 10" (25.5cm). Bind off all
stitches.

Felt the pieces separately (see page 54 for felting instructions).
Lay flat to dry. Using an enlarged template, cut out 18 dove
shapes. Sew together using whip stitch (page 65), leaving an
opening. Stuff with toy stuffing and sew closed.

Hang using ornament hooks or by making twisted
cord as follows:

Cut 2 15" [38cm] strands of yarn for
each Turtle Dove. With a friend holding
one end still, twist the end of one strand of
yarn clockwise until it begins twist onto itself.
Fold in half and let it twist onto itself. Tie a knot at
each end to prevent unraveling. Thread through the
whip stitch of ornament and tie together. Or simply
hang up each Turtle Dove with yarn.

Scarves to Impress

I end up with a lot of leftover yarn, and I find comfort in using it up! If you have discontinued yarn or just a small amount of yarn, these scarves come to the rescue. The first two use discontinued colors, but the whole idea is to be creative! Throw different weights of yarn together from your stash, and try to keep the colors from clashing. Muted tones work great for this.

The last scarf only uses 5¼oz. (150g) of the new Dreadlocks by Fleece Artist from Nova Scotia. If you haven't discovered their yarns, you are in for a treat!

SKILL LEVEL
Experienced

SIZE
SCARF #1
8" x 58½" (20cm x 149cm)

SCARF #2
4¾" x 62" (12cm x 157.5cm)

SCARF #3
8" x 60" (20.5cm x 152.5cm)

MATERIALS
SCARF #1
1 hank Fleece artist Dreadlocks (8¾ oz [250g]/200 yds [180m]; 78% mohair, 13% wool, 9% nylon looped mohair) Marine, (6) super bulky

1 pair US 17 (12mm) needles or size required to obtain gauge

SCARF #2
1 ball each of 4 colors of scrap yarn. Shown in Classic Elite La Gran (1½ oz [42g]/90 yds [82m]; 76 ½% mohair, 17 ½% wool, 6% nylon, #6542 Lavender Ice; Classic Elite Bravo (1¾ oz [50g]/48 yds [44m]; 40% rayon, 35% mohair, 13% silk, 6% wool, 6% nylon) #3736 Pink Champagne; and Classic Elite Zelda (1¾ oz [50g]/85 yds [78m]; 70% wool, 30% linen) #3650 Banana, discontinued, and #3601 Cotton Candy discontinued, (5) bulky

1 pair US 10 (6mm) needles or size required to obtain gauge

SCARF #3
1 hank Fleece Artist Baby Alpaca (8¾ oz [250g]/360 yds [330m]; 50% alpaca, 50% wool) Pale Yellow, (5) bulky

1 pair US 10 (6mm) needles or size required to obtain gauge

GAUGE
SCARF #1
8 stitches = 4" (10cm) in pattern

SCARF #2
16 stitches = 4" (10cm) in pattern

SCARF #3
13 stitches = 4" (10cm) in pattern.

Scarf #1

Cast on 15 stitches.

Knit 2 rows, then proceed as follows:

Rows 1 and 3 (WS) Purl.

Row 2 K1, *yo, k2tog; repeat from * to end of row.

Row 4 *Ssk, yo; repeat from * to last stitch, k1.

Repeat rows 1–4 until the Scarf measures 58½" (148.5cm) from the cast-on edge.

Knit 2 rows. Bind off all stitches.

FRINGE

Cut 2 strands of yarn 14" (35.5cm) long and attach at the edge. Repeat for every inch (2.5cm) along the cast-on and bind off edges. Do not trim.

Scarf #2:

Cast on 19 stitches.

Row 1 (WS) P4, k11, p4.

Row 2 K4, p11, k4.

Row 3 P2, p2tog, p11, p2togtbl, p2—17 stitches.

Row 4 K2, ssk, k9, k2tog, k2. 15 stitches.

Row 5 P2, p2tog, p7, p2togtbl, p2—13 stitches.

Row 6 K4, (yo, k1) 5 times, yo, k4—19 stitches.

Repeat rows 1–6 for pattern 23 more times (or to desired length), changing color at each repeat. Bind off all stitches.

FRINGE

Make fringe as for Scarf #1.

Scrap Yarn

When making a scarf out of scrap yarn, experiment with different yarns—try using larger needles than the ball band suggests, which will give the scarf a wispy, airy look. To further clean your stash of yarns you will never use, there are plenty of charitable groups that will be all too happy to take it off your hands.

Scarf #3

Cast on 25 stitches.

Work 1½" (4cm) in garter stitch (knit every row), ending with a WS facing for next row.

Row 1 and All WS Rows Purl.

Row 2 K1, *yo, k2tog; repeat form * to end of row.

Row 4 *Ssk, yo; repeat from * to last stitch, k1.

Repeat rows 1–4 until the Scarf measures 58½" (148.5cm) from the cast-on edge.

Work 1½" (4cm) in garter stitch. Bind off all stitches.

BORDER (OPTIONAL)

Pick up and knit 190 stitches along one side. Work 1½" (4cm) in garter stitch (knit every row), ending with a WS facing for next row. Bind off knitwise. Repeat for the other side.

FRINGE

Make fringe as for Scarf #1.

DECEMBER

IT WAS IN DECEMBER that I left Canada to live in Wales. I had arrived in London at night, and it couldn't have been more appropriate to drive into Wales, to my parents' home, on the blackest of Dylan Thomas's nights.

I was enthralled! There were cobblestone streets! In this new country, I would soon become more passionate about knitting and discover the wonderful knitting community and a plethora of yarn available to me. This would, in turn, give me the inspiration to design knitwear. I began collecting yarn, patterns, and books. I fell in love with Rowan Yarns. I experimented with substituting yarns and began to knit furiously. I made gifts for others as well as myself.

December is the month that gives us the magic of knitting. Whether for gifts or charity, it is with love that we knit this month. Let the yarn run through your fingers and savor the memories you're creating.

146

151

155

Blessed is he who expects nothing, for he shall never be disappointed.
—ALEXANDER POPE
(1688–1744)

Evening Festivities Cardigan

Everyone needs a little something to take the chill off a formal winter's evening. Rowan Kid Silk Haze's shimmer will set off your little black dress. I would also wear this wrapped and belted or with a brooch.

Intermediate

SIZE
Small (Medium, Large, X-Large)

Bust: 30 (34, 38, 42)" (76 [86.5, 96.5, 106.5]cm)

Finished size: 32 (36, 40, 45)" (81.5 [91.5, 101.5, 114.5]cm)

MATERIALS
6 (7, 8, 9) balls Rowan Kid Silk Haze (1 oz [25g]/227 yds [207m]; 67% super kid mohair, 18% silk, 10% polyester, 5% nylon) #605 Smoke, (3) light

1 pair US 6 (4mm) needles or size required to achieve gauge

1 36" (90cm) US 6 (4mm) circular needle

2 stitch holders.

GAUGE
24 stitches and 28 rows = 4" (10cm) in stockinette stitch

21 stitches and 32 rows = 4" (10cm) in Pattern Stitch

STITCH PATTERN
HOLIDAY LACE STITCH

Row 1 (RS): Knit.
Row 2 and All WS Rows: Purl.
Row 3: K3, *yo, sl1, k1, psso, k6; repeat from * to last 4 stitches, yo, sl1, k1, psso, k2.
Row 5: K1, *k2tog, yo, k1, yo, sl1, k1, psso, k3; repeat from

* to last 6 stitches, k2tog, yo, k1, yo, sl1, k1, psso, k1.
Row 7: As for row 3.
Row 9: Knit.
Row 11: K7, *yo, sl1, k1, psso, k6; repeat from * to end.
Row 13: K5, *k2tog, yo, k1, yo, sl1, k1, psso, k3; repeat from * to last 2 stitches, k2.
Row 15: As for row 11.
Row 16: Purl.
Repeat rows 1–16 for Holiday Lace Stitch.

Note The instructions are written for the smallest size. When changes are necessary for larger sizes, those instructions are enclosed in parentheses.

Left Front

**With straight needles, cast on 67 (75, 83, 91) stitches.

Row 1 (RS) K1, *p1, k1; repeat from * to end.

Repeat row 1 for seed stitch for ¾" (2cm), ending with RS facing for next row and increasing 4 stitches evenly across the last row. 71 (79, 87, 95) stitches.**

Work in Holiday Lace Stitch until the Left Front measures 8 (9, 10, 11)" (20.5 [23, 25.5, 28]cm) from the cast-on edge, ending with WS facing for next row.

Sizes S, M, and L Only Decrease 1 stitch at the beginning of the needle (front opening) on next and every 4th row to 65 (71, 85) stitches.

All Sizes Decrease 1 stitch at the beginning of the needle (front opening) on next and every 2nd row from previous decrease to 60 (70, 72, 79) stitches, ending with RS facing for next row.

ARMHOLE SHAPING
Next Row Bind off 6 stitches, work in pattern to end—54 (64, 66, 73) stitches.

Continue in Holiday Lace Stitch, decreasing 1 stitch at the armhole on the next 4 (6, 11, 15) rows AT THE SAME TIME, continue to decrease 1 stitch every 2nd row at the front opening until there are 18 (19, 20, 22) stitches.

Continue in Holiday Lace Stitch until the armhole measures 9 (9½, 10, 10½)" (23 [24, 25.5, 26.5]cm), ending with row 8 or 16, RS facing for next row.

SHOULDER SHAPING
Bind off 7 (7, 8, 9) stitches at the beginning of the next and following alternate row.

Work 1 row even. Bind off remaining stitches.

Right Front

Work from ** to ** as given for the Left Front.

Work in Holiday Lace Stitch until the Right Front measures 8 (9, 10, 11)" (20.5 [23, 25.5, 28]cm) from the cast-on edge, ending with WS facing for next row.

Next Row—Sizes S, M, and L Only: Decrease 1 stitch at the beginning of the needle (front opening) on next and every 4th row to 65 (71, 85) stitches.

All sizes: Decrease 1 stitch at the beginning of the needle (front opening) every 2nd row from previous decrease to 60 (70, 72, 79) stitches, ending with WS facing for next row.

ARMHOLE SHAPING

Next Row Bind off 6 stitches, work in pattern to end—54 (64, 66, 73) stitches.

Continue in Holiday Lace Stitch, decreasing 1 stitch at the armhole on the next 4 (6, 11, 15) rows AT THE SAME TIME, continue to decrease 1 stitch every 2nd row at the front opening until there are 18 (19, 20, 22) stitches.

Continue in Holiday Lace Stitch until the armhole measures 9 (9½, 10, 10½)" (23 [24, 25.5, 26.5]cm), ending with row 1 or 9, WS facing for next row.

SHOULDER SHAPING

Bind off 7 (7, 8, 9) stitches at the beginning of the next and following 2nd row.

Work 1 row even. Bind off remaining stitches.

Back

With straight needles, cast on 79 (89, 99, 113) stitches. Work in seed stitch as given for Left Front, increasing 8 (6, 4, 6) stitches evenly across the last row—87 (95, 103, 119) stitches.

Work in Holiday Lace Stitch until the Back measures the same as the Front to the armhole shaping, ending with RS facing for next row.

ARMHOLE SHAPING

Bind off 6 stitches at the beginning of the next 2 rows—75 (83, 91, 107) stitches.

Continuing in Holiday Lace Stitch, decrease 1 stitch at each end of the needle on the next 4 (6, 11, 15) rows—67 (71, 69, 77) stitches.

Continue in Holiday Lace Stitch until the armhole measures 9 (9½, 10, 10½)" (23 [24, 25.5, 26.5]cm), ending with row 8 or 16, RS facing for next row.

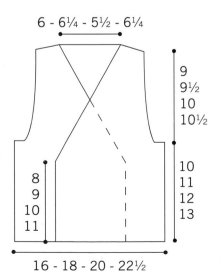

6 - 6¼ - 5½ - 6¼

9
9½
10
10½

10
11
12
13

8
9
10
11

16 - 18 - 20 - 22½

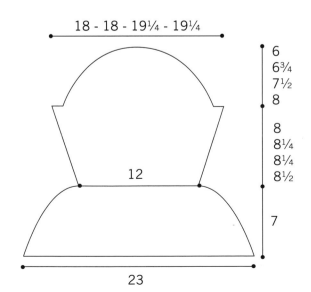

18 - 18 - 19¼ - 19¼

6
6¾
7½
8

8
8¼
8¼
8½

12

7

23

SHOULDER SHAPING

Bind off 7 (7, 8, 9) stitches at the beginning of the next 4 rows, then bind off 4 (5, 4, 4) stitches at the beginning of the next 2 rows. Leave the remaining 31 (33, 29, 33) stitches on a stitch holder for Back neck.

Sleeves (Make 2)

With straight needles, cast on 121 stitches. Work in seed stitch as given for the Back for ¾" (2cm), increasing 6 stitches evenly across the last row—127 stitches.

SLEEVE EDGING

Work in Holiday Lace Stitch for 7" (18cm), ending with row 8 or 16, RS facing for next row and decrease 1 stitch at center of last row—126 stitches.

Next Row *K2tog; repeat from * to end of row. 63 stitches.

Continuing in Holiday Lace Stitch, increase 1 stitch at each end of the needle every 2nd row to 85 (85, 87, 87) stitches, then every 4th row to 95 (95, 101, 101) stitches.

Continue in Holiday Lace Stitch until the Sleeve measures 8 (8¼, 8¼, 8¼, 8½)" (20.5 [21, 21, 21]cm) from the edging, ending with RS facing for next row.

SLEEVE CAP

Bind off 6 stitches at the beginning of the next 2 rows—83 (83, 89, 89) stitches.

Continuing in Holiday Lace Stitch, decrease 1 stitch at each end of the needle on next and every 2nd row 8 (12, 13, 17) times to 65 (57, 61, 53) stitches, then every row 22 (18, 20, 16) times to 21 stitches.

Bind off 2 stitches at the beginning of the next 4 rows—13 stitches. Bind off all stitches.

Finishing

Block the pieces to the measurements. Sew the shoulder seams.

NECK EDGING

With WS facing and circular needle, pick up and knit 135 stitches up the Left Front edge. Knit across 31 (33, 29, 33) stitches of Back neck stitch holder, decreasing 1 stitch at the center. Pick up and knit 135 stitches down the Right Front edge—301 (303, 299, 303) stitches.

Row 1 (WS) Knit.

Row 2 K1, *M1R, k1; repeat from * to end.

Row 3 Purl.

Row 4 Knit.

Continue in stockinette stitch for 2" (5cm), ending with RS facing for next row. Bind off all stitches purlwise.

Sew the side and sleeve seams.

Red Cable Cardigan

Nothing speaks to me like a red cabled knit. We tried this with a brown leather belt, which looked equally fetching and gave it a more casual look.

Experienced

SIZE
Bust: 30–32 (34–36, 38–40, 42–44)" (76–81 [86–91, 97–102, 107–112]cm)

Finished chest/bust: 36 (40, 44, 48)" (91 [102, 111, 122]cm)

MATERIALS
14 (14, 15, 15) balls Mission Falls 1824 Wool (1¾ oz [50g]/85 yds [78m]; 100% Merino Superwash Wool) #11 Red, (4) medium

1 pair US 7 (4.5mm) needles

1 pair US 8 (5mm) needles or size required to obtain gauge

1 cable needle

3 stitch holders

Six 7/8" (23mm) buttons

GAUGE
18 stitches and 24 rows = 4" (10cm) in stockinette stitch with larger needles

21 stitches and 26 rows = 4" (10cm) in Cable Pattern with larger needles

Note The instructions are written for the smallest size. When changes are necessary for larger sizes, those instructions are enclosed in parentheses.

> ## Gauge of Cable Patterns
>
> **The gauge of cables can be a tricky thing. You and I may have the same gauge in stockinette stitch, but we may cable at completely different tensions. How relaxed or tense you are doing cables will determine how your cables will look on the garment. I give both stockinette stitch and cable gauges in the pattern, and it is the latter that is the most important. Play with needle sizes to ensure you get a good fit.**

Back

With smaller needles, cast on 90 (94, 102, 114) stitches.

Row 1 (RS) K2, *p2, k2; repeat from * to end of row.

Row 2 P2, *k2, p2; repeat from * to end of row.

Repeat rows 1–2 for ribbing for 2¼" (5.5cm), increasing 6 (10, 10, 14) stitches evenly across the last row and ending with RS facing for next row—96 (104, 112, 128) stitches.

Change to larger needles and proceed as follows:

Row 1 (RS) (K2, p2) 2 (3, 4, 6) times, p2, c2b, p2, k4, c4b, c4f, k4, p2, c2b, p2, (c2b, c2f, p2, c2b, p2) 3 times, k4, c4b, c4f, k4, p2, c2b, p2, (k2, p2) 2 (3, 4, 6) times.

Row 2 and All WS Rows Knit the knit stitches and purl the purl stitches.

Row 3 (P2, k2) 2 (3, 4, 6) times, p2, c2f, p2, k2, c4b, k4, c4f, k2, p2, c2f, p2, (c2f, c2b, p2, c2f, p2) 3 times, k2, c4b, k4, c4f, k2, p2, c2f, p2, (p2, k2) 2 (3, 4, 6) times.

Row 5 (K2, p2) 2 (3, 4, 6) times, p2, c2b, p2, c4b, k8, c4f, p2, c2b, p2, (c2b, c2f, p2, c2b, p2) 3 times, c4b, k8, c4f, p2, c2b, p2, (k2, p2) 2 (3, 4, 6) times.

Row 7 (P2, k2) 2 (3, 4, 6) times, p2, c2f, p2, k4, c4b, c4f, k4, p2, c2f, p2, (c2f, c2b, p2, c2f, p2) 3 times, k4, c4b, c4f, k4, p2, c2f, p2, (p2, k2) 2 (3, 4, 6) time(s).

Row 9 (K2, p2) 2 (3, 4, 6) times, p2, c2b, p2, k2, c4b, k4, c4f, k2, p2, c2b, p2, (c2b, c2f, p2, c2b, p2) 3 times, k2, c4b, k4, c4f, k2, p2, c2b, p2, (k2, p2) 2 (3, 4, 6) times.

Row 11 (P2, k2) 2 (3, 4, 6) times, p2, c2f, p2, c4b, k8, c4f, p2, c2f, p2, (c2f, c2b, p2, c2f, p2) 3 times, c4b, k8, c4f, p2, c2f, p2, (p2, k2) 2 (3, 4, 6) times.

Row 12 Knit the knit stitches and purl the purl stitches.

Repeat rows 1–12 for pattern.

Work in pattern until the Back measures 17¼ (18½, 19, 19½)" (44 [47, 48.25, 49.5]cm) from the cast-on edge, ending with RS facing for next row.

ARMHOLE SHAPING

Bind off 4 (5, 5, 8) stitches at the beginning of the next 4 rows—80 (84, 92, 96) stitches.

Continue even in pattern until the armhole measures 8¼ (8½, 9, 9½)" (21 [21.5, 23, 24]cm), ending with RS facing for next row.

SHOULDER SHAPING

Bind off 7 (8, 9, 10) stitches at the beginning of the next 4 rows, then 8 (8, 10, 10) stitches at the beginning of the following 2 rows. Leave the remaining 36 stitches on a stitch holder.

Left Front

**With smaller needles cast on 42 (46, 50, 58) stitches.

Work in ribbing as given for the Back for 2¼" (5.5cm), increasing 4 stitches evenly across the last row, ending with RS facing for next row—46 (50, 54, 62) stitches.**

Row 1 (RS) (K2, p2) 1 (2, 3, 5) time(s), p2, c2b, p2, k4, c4b, c4f, k4, p2, c2b, p2, c2b, c2f, p2, (c2f, p2) twice.

Row 2 and All WS Rows Knit the knit stitches and purl the purl stitches.

Row 3 (P2, k2) 1 (2, 3, 5) times, p2, c2f, p2, k2, c4b, k4, c4f, k2, p2, c2f, p2, c2f, c2b, p2, (c2f, p2) twice.

Row 5 (K2, p2) 1 (2, 3, 5) times, p2, c2b, p2, c4b, k8, c4f, p2, c2b, p2, c2b, c2f, p2, (c2b, p2) twice.

Row 7 (P2, k2) 1 (2, 3, 5) times, p2, c2f, p2, k4, c4b, c4f, k4, p2, c2f, p2, c2f, c2b, p2, (c2f, p2) twice.

Row 9 (K2, p2) 1 (2, 3, 5) times, p2, c2b, p2, k2, c4b, k4, c4f, k2, p2, c2b, p2, c2b, c2f, p2, (c2b, p2) twice.

Row 11 (P2, k2) 1 (2, 3, 5) times, p2, c2f, p2, c4b, k8, c4f, p2, c2f, p2, c2f, c2b, p2, (c2f, p2) twice.

Row 12 Knit the knit stitches and purl the purl stitches.

Repeat rows 1–12 rows for pattern.

Work in pattern as given above until the Left Front measures

17¼ (18½, 19, 19½)" (44, 47, 48, 49.5cm) from the cast-on edge, ending with RS facing for next row.

ARMHOLE SHAPING

Bind off 4 (5, 5, 8) stitches at the beginning of next and following alternate row, working in pattern to end of row—38 (40, 44, 46) stitches. Continue in pattern until the Left Front measures 23½ (25, 26, 27)" (59.5 [63.5, 66, 68.5]cm) from the cast-on edge, ending with WS facing for next row.

NECK SHAPING

Next Row Work in pattern for 4 stitches. Slip these 4 stitches onto a stitch holder (neck edge). Work in pattern to end of row.

Decrease 1 stitch at the neck edge on every row to 22 (24, 28, 30) stitches. Continue even in pattern until the armhole measures 8¼ (8½, 9, 9½)" (21 [21.5, 23, 24]cm), ending with RS facing for next row.

SHOULDER SHAPING

Bind off 7 (8, 9, 10) stitches at the beginning of the next and 2nd row. Work 1 row even, then bind off remaining 8 (8, 10, 10) stitches.

Right Front

Work from ** to ** as given for Left Front. Change to larger needles and proceed in pattern as follows:

Row 1 (RS) P2, (c2b, p2) twice, c2b, c2f, p2, c2b, p2, k4, c4b, c4f, k4, p2, c2b, p2, (k2, p2) 1 (2, 3, 5) times.

Row 2 and All WS Rows Knit the knit stitches and purl the purl stitches.

Row 3 P2, (c2f, p2) twice, c2f, c2b, p2, c2f, p2, k2, c4b, k4, c4f, k2, p2, c2f, p2, (p2, k2) 1 (2, 3, 5) times.

Row 5 P2, (c2b, p2) twice, c2b, c2f, p2, c2b, p2, c4f, k8, c4f, p2, c2b, p2 (k2, p2) 1 (2, 3, 5) times.

Row 7 P2, (c2f, p2) twice, c2f, c2b, p2, c2f, p2, k4, c4b, c4f, k4, p2, c2f, p2, (p2, k2) 1 (2, 3, 5) times.

Row 9 P2, (c2b, p2) twice, c2b, c2f, p2, c2b, p2, k2, c4b, k4, c4f, k2, p2, c2b, p2, (k2, p2) 1 (2, 3, 5) times.

Row 11 P2, (c2f, p2) twice, c2f, c2b, p2, c2f, p2, c4f, k8, c4f, p2, c2f, p2, (p2, k2) 1 (2, 3, 5) times.

Row 12 Knit the knit stitches and purl the purl stitches.

Repeat rows 1–12 for pattern.

Work in pattern until the Right Front measures 17¼ (18½, 19, 19½)" (44, 47, 48, 49.5cm) from the cast-on edge, ending with WS facing for next row.

ARMHOLE SHAPING

Bind off 4 (5, 5, 8) stitches at the beginning of next and following alternate row, work in pattern to end of row—38 (40, 44, 46) stitches.

Continue in pattern until the Right Front measures 23½ (25, 26, 27)" (59.5 [63.5, 66, 68.5]cm) from the cast-on edge, ending with RS facing for next row.

NECK SHAPING

Next Row Work in pattern for 4 stitches. Slip these 4 stitches onto a stitch holder (neck edge). Work in pattern to end of row.

Decrease 1 stitch at the neck edge every row to 22 (24, 28, 30) stitches. Continue even in pattern until the armhole measures 8¼ (8½, 9, 9½)" (21 [21.5, 23, 24]cm), ending with WS facing for next row.

SHOULDER SHAPING

Bind off 7 (8, 9, 10) stitches at the beginning of the next and following alternate row.

Work 1 row even, then bind off remaining 8 (8, 10, 10) stitches.

Sleeves (Make 2)

With smaller needles, cast on 46 (46, 46, 50) stitches.

Work in ribbing as given for the Back for 2¼" (5.5cm),

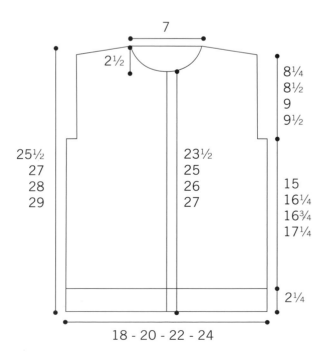

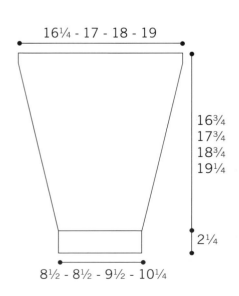

increasing 2 (2, 4, 6) stitches evenly across the last row—48 (48, 50, 56) stitches.

Change to larger needles and proceed in pattern as follows:

Row 1 (RS) P0 (0, 0, 2), k0 (0, 1, 2), p2, c2b, p2, c2b, c2f, p2, c2b, p2, k4, c4b, c4f, k4, p2, c2b, p2, c2b, c2f, p2, c2b, p2, k0 (0, 1, 2), p0 (0, 0, 2).

Row 2 and All WS Rows Knit the knit stitches and purl the purl stitches.

Row 3 Cast on 1 stitch using cable cast-on method (page xx), k0 (0, 0, 2), p0 (0, 1, 2), p2, c2f, p2, c2f, c2b, p2, c2f, p2, k2, c4b, k4, c4f, k2, p2, c2f, p2, c2f, c2b, p2, c2f, p2, p0 (0, 1, 2), k0 (0, 0, 2), kf&b—50 (50, 52, 58) stitches.

Row 5 P0 (0, 0, 3), k1 (1, 2, 2), p2, c2b, p2, c2b, c2f, p2, c2b, p2, c4b, k8, c4f, p2, c2b, p2, c2b, c2f, p2, c2b, p2, k1 (1, 2, 2), p0 (0, 0, 3).

Row 7 Cast on 1 stitch using cable cast-on method (page 70), k0 (0, 0, 3), p1 (1, 2, 2), p2, c2f, p2, c2f, c2b, p2, c2f, p2, k4, c4b, c4f, k4, p2, c2f, p2, c2f, c2b, p2, c2f, p2, p1 (1, 2, 2), p0 (0, 0, 3), kf&b—52 (52, 54, 60) stitches.

Row 9 P0 (0, 0, 2), k0 (0, 1, 2), p4, c2b, p2, c2b, c2f, p2, c2b, p2, k2, c4b, k4, c4f, k2, p2, c2b, p2, c2b, c2f, p2, c2b, p4, k0 (0, 1, 2), p0 (0, 0, 2).

Row 11 P0 (0, 0, 2), k0 (0, 1, 2), p4, c2f, p2, c2f, c2b, p2, c2f, p2, c4b, k8, c4f, p2, c2f, p2, c2f, c2b, p2, c2f, p4, k0 (0, 1, 2), p0 (0, 0, 2).

Row 12 Knit the knit stitches and purl the purl stitches.

Repeat rows 1–12 for pattern.

Working in pattern, continue to increase 1 stitch at each end of the needle on every 4th row to 62 (72, 76, 82) stitches, then every following 6th row to 84 (88, 92, 96) stitches, taking increased stitches into pattern.

Continue in pattern even until the Sleeve measures 19¾ (20, 20, 20)" (50 [51, 51, 51]cm) from the cast-on edge, ending with RS facing for next row. Bind off all stitches.

Belt

With smaller needles, cast on 9 stitches.

Row 1 (RS) K1, (k1b, p1) 3 times, k1b, k1.

Row 2 (K1, p1b) 4 times, k1.

Repeat rows 1–2 until the Belt measures 58" (147.5cm), ending with row 2. Bind off all stitches.

Finishing

Pin all pieces to measurements and cover with a damp cloth. Leave the cloth to dry on the garment.

BUTTONHOLE BAND

With RS of work facing and smaller needles, pick up and knit 130 (134, 142, 146) stitches along the Right Front edge from the cast-on edge to the neck edge.

Beginning with row 2, work 3 rows in ribbing as given for the Back.

Row 4 (RS): Work in ribbing for 4 (4, 5, 4) stitches, *yfwd, k2tog, work in ribbing for 22 (23, 24, 25) stitches; repeat from * 4 more times, yfwd, k2tog, work in ribbing to end of row.

Work 3 rows in ribbing, ending with RS facing for next row.

Bind off in ribbing.

BUTTON BAND

Work as for Buttonhole Band, working ribbing for row 4 instead of making buttonholes.

BELT LOOPS (MAKE 2; OPTIONAL)

With 4mm crochet hook, ch 10. Work 1 row of sc. Fasten off. Attach each end to side of cardigan at waistline.

COLLAR

Sew the shoulder seams. With RS of work facing and smaller needles, beginning at the center of the top edge of the buttonhole band, pick up and knit 3 stitches, knit across the 4 stitches on the Right Front stitch holder, pick up and knit 15 stitches up the Right Front neck edge, knit across 36 stitches from the back neck stitch holder, decreasing 2 stitches evenly across, pick up and knit 15 stitches down the Left Front neck edge, knit across the 4 stitches on the Left Front stitch holder, pick up and knit 3 stitches to the center of the top edge of the Button Band. 80 stitches. Beginning with row 2, work ribbing as given for the Back for 5" (12.5cm). Bind off in ribbing.

Sew in the sleeves. Sew the side and sleeve seams. Sew on the buttons, matching them to the buttonholes.

Chill Out! Cable Hat

While this beginner pattern has cables, I firmly believe they are not as difficult as they look and a small project, like this, is the perfect place to dive in!

Beginner

SIZE
To fit an average-size woman's head

Approximately 22" (56cm) around base of hat

MATERIALS
2 balls Needful Yarns Feeling (³⁄₄ oz [25g]/154 yds [140m]; 70% wool/20% Silk/10% Cashmere), #12940 Plum, ③ light

1 set of 4 US 6 (4mm) double-pointed needles or size required to achieve gauge

GAUGE
41 stitches and 26 rows = 4" (10cm) in Cable Stitch.

STITCH PATTERN
CABLE STITCH
Rnd 1: *P2, k4; repeat from * to end of row.
Rnd 2: *P2, c4b; repeat from * to end of row.
Rnds 3–6: Repeat rnd 1.
Repeat rounds 1–6 for Cable Stitch.

Hat

Cast on 174 stitches and divide evenly on 3 needles (58 stitches on each needle). Join to work in the round.

Work in Cable Stitch until the hat measures 6½" (16.5cm) from the cast-on edge, ending with rnd 3 of pattern facing for next row.

HAT TOP

Rnd 1 *P2tog, c4b. Repeat from * to end of row—145 stitches.

Work 3 rounds even in pattern.

Rnd 5 *K2tog, k3; repeat from * to end of row—116 stitches.

Work 2 rounds even in pattern.

Rnd 8 *C4b; repeat from * to end of row.

Rnd 9 *K2tog, k2; repeat from * to end of row—87 stitches.

Rnd 10 Knit.

Rnd 11 *K2tog, k1; repeat from * to end of row—58 stitches.

Rnd 12 Knit.

Rnd 13 *K2tog; repeat from * to end of row—29 stitches.

Rnd 14 K1, *k2tog; repeat from * to end of row—14 stitches.

Break the yarn, leaving a long end. Draw the yarn through the remaining stitches and pull tight.

RESOURCES

The yarns chosen for the book should be available at your local yarn shop or online. If you cannot find them, or for more information and distribution of the yarns used for the projects, please contact the following companies:

BLUE SKY ALPACAS, INC.

PO Box 88

Cedar, MN 55011

763-753-5815

888-460-8862

CLASSIC ELITE YARNS

122 Western Avenue

Lowell, MA 01851-1434

978-453-2837

www.classiceliteyarns.com

CRYSTAL PALACE

160 23rd Street

Richmond, California 94804

cpyinfo@straw.com

www.straw.com

FLEECE ARTIST

kathryn@fleeceartist.com

Fax: (902) 462-0800

www.fleeceartist.com

MANOS DEL URUGUAY

In Canada:

334 Ottawa St. N.

Hamilton, Ontario

L8H, 4A1, Canada

905-544-0699

866-919-0995

www.ashleyyarns.com

E-mail: letha_burden@cogeco.ca

In the United States:

PO Box 770, Medford, MA 02155

888-566-9970

Tel: 905-544-YARN (9276)

877-GET-WOOL (438-9665)

MISSION FALLS

CNS Yarns

5333 Casgrain #1204

Montreal, QC

H2T 1X3

877-244-1204

www.missionfalls.com

NEEDFUL YARNS

In Canada:

4476 Chesswood Drive Unit 10, 11

Toronto, Ontario, Canada M3J 2B9

416, 398, 3700 Fax 416, 398, 5300

In the United States:

60 Industrial Parkway PMB #233

Cheektowaga, NY 14227

866-800-4700

info@needfulyarnsinc.com

www.needfulyarnsinc.com

PATONS/LILY

Spinrite Yarns

320 Livingstone Avenue South

Listowel, ON

Canada

N4W 3H3

888-368-8401

www.spinriteyarns.com

www.sugarncream.com

www.patonsyarns.com

ROWAN

Westminster Fibers, Inc.

4 Townsend Avenue, Unit 8

Nashua, NH 03063

800-445-9276

www.westminsterfibers.com

SR KERTZER FOR BUTTERFLY AND ALAFOSS

50 Trowers Road

Woodbridge, ON

L4L 7K6

Canada

800-263-2354

info@kertzer.com

www.kertzer.com

TAHKI

Tahki • Stacy Charles, Inc.

70-30 80th St. Building 36

Ridgewood, NY 11385

800-338-YARN

info@tahkistacycharles.com

www.tahkistacycharles.com

STANDARD YARN WEIGHT SYSTEM

Yarn Weight Symbol and Category names	1 SUPER FINE	2 FINE	3 LIGHT	4 MEDIUM	5 BULKY	6 SUPER BULKY
Type of Yarns in Category	Sock, Fingerling, Baby	Sport, Baby	DK, Light Worsted	Worsted, Afghan, Aran	Chunky, Craft, Rug	Bulky, Roving
Knit Gauge Range* in Stockinette Stitch to 4 inches (10 cm)	27–32 sts	23–26 sts	21–24 st	16–20 sts	12–15 sts	6–11 sts
Recommended Needle in Metric Size Range	2.25–3.25 mm	3.25–3.75 mm	3.75–4.5 mm	4.5–5.5 mm	5.5–8 mm	8 mm and larger
Recommended Needle in U.S. Size Range	1 to 3	3 to 5	5 to 7	7 to 9	9 to 11	11 and larger
Crochet Gauge* Ranges in Single Crochet to 4 inches (10 cm)	21–32 sts	16–20 sts	12–17 st	11–14 sts	8–11 sts	5–9 sts
Recommended Hook in Metric Size Range	2.25–3.25 mm	3.5–4.4 mm	4.5–5.5 mm	5.5–6.5 mm	6.5–9 mm	9 mm and larger
Recommended Hook in U.S. Size Range	B-1 to E-4	E-4 to 7	7 to 1-9	1-9 to K-$10\frac{1}{2}$	K-$10\frac{1}{2}$ to M-13	M-13 and larger

* Guidelines Only: *The above reflect the most commonly used gauges and needle or hook sizes for specific yarn categories.*

GLOSSARY

c2b (c2f) = Slip the next stitch onto a cable needle and hold at the back (front) of the work. K1, then k1 from the cable needle.

c4b (c4f) = Slip the next 2 stitches onto a cable needle and hold at the back (front) of the work. K2, then k2 from the cable needle.

c2l = Knit into back of the 2nd stitch on the left-hand needle, then without removing the stitch, knit into the front of the 1st stitch on the left-hand needle, slipping both off at the same time.

c5r = Slip the next stitch onto a cable needle and hold at the back of the work. Knit 4 stitches from the left-hand needle, then knit the stitch from the cable needle.

c5l = Slip the next 4 stitches onto a cable needle and hold at the front of the work. Knit the next stitch from the left-hand needle, then knit the stitches from the cable needle.

CC = Contrast color.

ch = chain.

dc = Double crochet.

garter stitch = Knit every row.

hdc = Half double crochet.

Inc1P = Increase 1 stitch purlwise by purling into the front and back of the next stitch.

k = Knit.

k1b = Knit in to the back of the stitch.

k1f&b = knit into the front and then the back of the stitch

k1f&bf = knit into the front, back, and front of the same stitch

k2tog = knit 2 together.

k2togtbl = knit 2 together through back loop

MC = Main color.

M1P = Make 1 stitch by picking up the strand between stitches and purling into the back of this loop.

M1R = Make 1 right-leaning stitch by picking up the strand between stitches from back to front and knitting it.

M1L (M1) = Make 1 left-leaning stitch by picking up the strand between stitches from front to back and knitting it through the back loop.

p = Purl.

p1b = Purl into the back of the stitch.

reverse stockinette stitch = Purl RS rows; knit WS rows. (Purl every round when working in the round.)

rnd = Round.

RS = Right side.

sc = Single crochet.

sl st = Slip stitch.

Sl1, k1, psso = Slip 1, knit 1, pass the slipped stitch over.

Ssk (slip, slip, knit) = Slip the next 2 stitches knitwise, one at a time. Place the left-hand needle through the front of these stitches and knit them together.

st = Stitch.

stockinette stitch = Knit RS rows; purl WS rows. (Knit every round when working in the round.)

t3f = Slip 2 stitches onto a cable needle and hold at the front of the work. P1 from the left-hand needle, then k2 from the cable needle.

t3b = Slip 1 stitch onto a cable needle and hold at the back of the work. K2 from the left-hand needle, then p1 from the cable needle.

T4f = Slip 2 stitches onto a cable needle and leave at the front of the work. P2 from the left-hand needle, then k2 from the cable needle.

t4b = Slip 2 stitches onto a cable needle and leave at the back of the work. K2 from the left-hand needle, then p2 from the cable needle.

t5r = Slip 1 stitch onto a cable needle and hold at the back of the work. Knit 4 stitches from the left-hand needle, then p1 from the cable needle.

t5l = Slip the next 4 stitches onto a cable needle and hold at the front of the work. Purl 1 stitch from the left-hand needle, then k4 from the cable needle.

WS = Wrong Side

yds = Yards

yfwd = Yarn forward around needle.

yfon = Yarn forward and over the needle.

yfrn = Yarn forward around needle.

yo = Yarn over.

INDEX

31901046200269